peaceful

on

purpose

The Power to Remain Calm, Strong, and Confident in Every Season

JOEL OSTEEN

New York • Nashville

ALSO BY JOEL OSTEEN

ALL THINGS ARE WORKING
FOR YOUR GOOD
*Daily Readings from All Things
Are Working for Your Good*

BLESSED IN THE DARKNESS
Blessed in the Darkness Journal
Blessed in the Darkness Study Guide

BREAK OUT!
Break Out! Journal
Daily Readings from Break Out!

EMPTY OUT THE NEGATIVE

EVERY DAY A FRIDAY
Every Day a Friday Journal
Daily Readings from Every Day a Friday

FRESH START
Fresh Start Study Guide

I DECLARE
I Declare Personal Application Guide

NEXT LEVEL THINKING
Next Level Thinking Journal
Next Level Thinking Study Guide
*Daily Readings from Next Level
Thinking*

PEACEFUL ON PURPOSE
Peaceful on Purpose Study Guide

THE ABUNDANCE MIND-SET

THE POWER OF FAVOR
The Power of Favor Study Guide

THE POWER OF I AM
The Power of I Am Journal
The Power of I Am Study Guide
Daily Readings from The Power of I Am

THINK BETTER, LIVE BETTER
Think Better, Live Better Journal
Think Better, Live Better Study Guide
*Daily Readings from Think Better,
Live Better*

TWO WORDS THAT WILL CHANGE
YOUR LIFE TODAY

WITH VICTORIA OSTEEN
Our Best Life Together
Wake Up to Hope Devotional

YOU CAN, YOU WILL
You Can, You Will Journal
Daily Readings from You Can, You Will

YOUR BEST LIFE NOW
Your Best Life Begins Each Morning
Your Best Life Now for Moms
Your Best Life Now Journal
Your Best Life Now Study Guide
Daily Readings from Your Best Life Now
*Scriptures and Meditations for
Your Best Life Now*
Starting Your Best Life Now

peaceful

on

purpose

FaithWords
Hachette Book Group
1290 Avenue of the Americas, New York, NY 10104
faithwords.com
twitter.com/faithwords

First Edition: May 2021

FaithWords is a division of Hachette Book Group, Inc. The FaithWords name and logo are trademarks of Hachette Book Group, Inc.

The publisher is not responsible for websites (or their content) that are not owned by the publisher.

The Hachette Speakers Bureau provides a wide range of authors for speaking events. To find out more, go to www.hachettespeakersbureau.com or call (866) 376-6591.

Library of Congress Control Number: 2020946384

ISBN: 978-1-4555-3439-5 (hardcover), 978-1-4555-3438-8 (ebook), 978-1-5460-1751-6 (large print), 978-1-5460-1762-2 (international trade)

Printed in the United States of America

LSC-H

Printing 1, 2021

CONTENTS

CHAPTER ONE

All Is Well

It's easy to go through life worried about the future, frustrated because a dream is taking so long to come to pass, upset because somebody did you wrong. But instead of complaining about the difficulty, instead of being upset because your plans didn't work out, instead of losing your peace and living frustrated, you need to remember this simple phrase: *All is well.* God is still on the throne. He's directing your steps. He wouldn't have allowed it unless He had a purpose. When you're tempted to get discouraged, keep reminding yourself that all is well. "I lost my biggest client, but I'm not stressed. I know something better is coming. All is well." "I was cheated in a business deal, but that's okay. God is my vindicator, so all is well." "I prayed for my loved one, but they didn't make it. I'm not bitter, because I know they're in Heaven rejoicing and free from pain. All is well." When you have this "all is well" attitude, there's a rest, a peace of mind. It takes the pressure off. You don't live on a roller coaster. You know all is well on the mountaintop, and all is well in the valley. All is well when business is great, and all is well when it's slow. You have a made-up mind. You know God is bigger than anything you're facing. As long as you're in faith, all the forces of darkness cannot stop you.

This is what the three Hebrew teenagers did in the book of Daniel. Shadrach, Meshach, and Abednego wouldn't bow down to the king's golden idol. When they were about to be thrown into the fiery furnace, they could have complained, "God, it's not fair. We serve You, and look what happens." Instead they said to the king, "We're not going to bow down. We know that our God will deliver us, but even if He doesn't, we're still not going to bow." They were saying, "All is well if it goes our way, and all is well if it doesn't go our way. All is well if our prayers get answered, and all is well if they don't get answered." The king had them thrown into the blazing furnace, and it should have killed them instantly. But when the king looked into the furnace, he said, "Didn't we throw three bound men into the fire? I see four men walking around, unbound and unharmed, and one looks like the Son of God." When you have this "all is well" attitude, the Creator of the universe will make things happen that you could never make happen.

> When you have this "all is well" attitude, the Creator of the universe will make things happen that you could never make happen.

As with these teenagers, you may be in a situation where

you don't see a way out. You could be worried, discouraged, and frustrated. You need to start declaring, "All is well." "My marriage is struggling, but I'm not living upset. All is well." "I'm dealing with this addiction, and I'm not where I thought I'd be in life, but I'm not discouraged. God is still working on me, and I'm not a finished product. All is well." "I never thought I'd be facing this sickness, or this bankruptcy, or this divorce, but can I tell you that all is well? I'm not worried. I'm not upset. I know God is in complete control."

Maybe you're still single, and you thought you would have met your spouse by now. Let me encourage you that all is well. God has the right person already lined up. They're in your future. It's not too late. Get in agreement with God. Don't go around thinking it's never going to happen. Have the attitude, *all is well*. Your child may have made some poor choices. Worrying is not going to help, and losing sleep is not going to change it. All through the day let *all is well* be in your thoughts. You'll hear that voice say, "What if he doesn't change?" Answer back, "All is well." "What if it doesn't work out?" "All is well." "What if he gets in more trouble?" "All is well."

Replace the thoughts of worry with *all is well*. The medical report may not have been good. It would be easy to let these negative words play over and over: *You're not going to make it. Learn to live with it.* No, turn off that recording and put on this new recording: *All is well. The number of my days, He will fulfill. Nothing can snatch me out of God's hands.* You may be in a legal battle. You don't like it, and it isn't fair, but you say, "All is well. The enemy will fall into the trap they set for me."

When you meditate on that, you're saying, "God, I trust You. You're bigger than this obstacle. You can turn any situation around."

It's Just a Weed

What's interesting is that the Hebrew teenagers were doing the right thing when the wrong thing happened to them. Being in God's perfect will doesn't mean you won't have difficulties. You can't reach your destiny without opposition, unfair situations, and people doing you wrong. When things come against you, it's easy to think, *All is not well. Look at these difficulties.* But the truth is, the enemy wouldn't be fighting you unless he knew that God has something amazing in front of you. In tough times you can say "all is well," knowing that the opposition is a sign that something great is coming. The Scripture says, "Don't think it strange when you face fiery trials." Don't get bent out of shape because life throws you a curve and you had an unexpected difficulty. Sometimes when you face challenges, it's not because you're doing something wrong, but because you're doing something right.

Sometimes when you face challenges, it's not because you're doing something wrong, but because you're doing something right.

Jesus told a parable about this in Matthew 13. A farmer went out and sowed wheat in his field. It was good seed. He was doing the right thing. But at night while he slept, an enemy snuck in and sowed weeds in his soil. When the seeds sprouted and began to grow, the weeds sprung up among the wheat. His workers asked, "Where did the weeds come from? You didn't sow these seeds." Anytime you're doing the right thing, you're honoring God, being productive, and helping others, don't be surprised if you find weeds among your wheat. As with this man, it doesn't mean you're doing anything wrong. You think, *I've been loyal to this company for twenty years. Why did they treat me badly? I've raised my children right, so why are they veering off course?* Those are simply weeds that the enemy has sowed into your field to try to discourage you, distract you, and get you off course. The good news is, those weeds cannot keep you from your destiny. If that trouble was going to stop God's plan for your life, He would never have permitted it. I've learned that the weeds always spring up right before the harvest. When your business slows down, or a child starts acting up, or you have trouble in a relationship, don't panic. You are close to your breakthrough. Your harvest is about to come. That's why those weeds are springing up.

Instead of falling apart and thinking, *I can't believe this is happening,* your attitude should be, *It's just another weed. No big deal. I didn't sow it. I don't have to reap it. God said He would take care of it.* If for some reason you are to get laid off from your job, don't panic. It's just a weed springing up. If you stay in faith, God will give you a better job. If you get a negative medical report, don't get discouraged and ask, "God, why me?" No, look at that sickness as a weed. It's not permanent; it's temporary. It can't keep you from your destiny. You're a child of the Most High God. Maybe a friend did you wrong and walked out of your relationship. The next time you see him or her, under your breath just say, "Hello, weed." You don't need them in order to become who God created you to be.

The parable ends with the workers asking the farmer, "Should we pull up the weeds?" He says, "No, just wait until it's time to harvest the wheat. At the right time they'll be destroyed." That's what God is saying to us. When weeds suddenly pop up in your life—the unexpected challenges, the sickness, the problem at work—you don't have to fight those battles. Don't spend all your time trying to pull up the weeds. You can't fix everything in your own strength. If you're constantly trying to straighten someone out, to fix a bad situation, or to resolve a problem, you're going to be frustrated. The Scripture says, "Those who have believed enter into the rest of God." At some point you have to say, "God, I'm trusting You to take care of my weeds. I didn't sow them,

> *If you're constantly trying to straighten someone out, to fix a bad situation, or to resolve a problem, you're going to be frustrated.*

and I know I don't have to reap them." You keep honoring God, being your best, and God will move the wrong people out of the way, He'll restore what's been stolen, and He'll straighten out the situation at work. The battle is not yours; the battle is the Lord's. Be still and know that He is God.

You shouldn't be constantly uptight, worried, rebuking, resisting, and trying to fix things. It takes a mature person to say, "Everything is not perfect. I have some struggles and some situations I wish were different, but can I tell you that all is well? I'm at peace. I'm not upset. I know at the right time God will remove the weeds. Until then I'm going to relax and enjoy my life."

First the Weed, Then the Harvest

Too often we get frustrated by difficulties, but you have to realize you can't have a harvest without a few weeds. David would never have ascended to the throne without that big weed named Goliath. Joseph would never have been second-in-command of Egypt without being betrayed by his own brothers and falsely accused of a crime. We would never have had the former Compaq Center without a three-and-a-half-year lawsuit. There are weeds in all our lives. You're not always going to understand where it came from or why it happened. Don't get discouraged. Just keep moving forward, knowing that all is well and God promises He'll take care of your weeds.

I know a young couple who had been saving money for over ten years to buy their first home. At one point everything came together. They found the house they wanted. They were so excited, but on the day they were to sign the contract, the wife was at the Realtor's office and about to finalize the details when she got a call from her husband saying he had just lost his job. He had worked for this company for six years, always done his best, and had a great attitude, but his supervisor didn't like him and had treated him unfairly for many years. What was that? A weed. Their wheat was about to come up, but first the weed popped up. They could have gotten discouraged and thought, *Just our luck. Right when it was about to happen.* No, they had this attitude: *All is well. God is in control. This is not a surprise to Him.* Rather than sit at home discouraged, when the husband wasn't out interviewing for a new job, he would come to Lakewood and volunteer. Week after week, it didn't look as though anything was happening on the job front. But when you see the weeds popping up—the unexpected challenges, the wrong thing happening when you were doing the right thing—you can be sure your harvest is getting closer.

> When you see the weeds popping up—the unexpected challenges, the wrong thing happening when you were doing the right thing—you can be sure your harvest is getting closer.

Five months later, this man got a call from his former company. He hadn't spoken to them since he was let go. An executive from the corporate headquarters informed him that they had fired his old supervisor and put in place a new management team. They wanted this young man to come back, and they not only offered him his old position but restored all his seniority, all his retirement benefits, and all his health benefits. And when the couple went back to check on the house they had wanted, it was still available, just as though it had been put on hold for them. Today he's not only excelling in his career, but they live in their dream house, and they're blessed and happy as can be.

This Is What Faith Is All About

In 2 Kings 4, Elisha prophesied to an older woman that she would have a child. She had been barren her whole life. A year later, she had a baby boy and was so excited. When the boy was about ten years old, he was out in the field playing one day when his head began to hurt. They carried him back to his home, and he died in his mother's arms. You can imagine how distraught and heartbroken she was. After waiting all those years, now her only son was gone. She determined immediately to go to Elisha for help, and when her husband asked if something was wrong, she only replied, "All is well." She said nothing about their son.

This woman saddled one of their donkeys and took off full speed toward Elisha's house in the mountains. Elisha saw her coming from a great distance, in such a big rush. He told his assistant, Gehazi, to run out to meet her on the road and see if anything was wrong. Gehazi met her on the path and said, "Elisha is wondering why you're coming unexpectedly and in such a hurry. Is everything okay with you? Is everything okay with your husband? Is everything okay with your son?" She answered back, "All is well." She kept going full steam until she reached Elisha.

"Well, Joel, I don't want to lie. If it's not well, I'm not going to say that it is well." But this is what faith is all about. The Scripture says, "...and calls things that are not as though they already were." When the situation doesn't look good, when you don't see how you can accomplish your dreams, when your child is running with the wrong crowd, every voice says, "It's not going to work out. It's too late. Just accept it." That's when you have to dig your heels in and say as this woman did, "All is well." That's not just being optimistic; you are prophesying your future. You are speaking faith into your destiny. Don't

> *Don't use your words to describe the situation; use your words to change the situation.*

use your words to describe the situation; use your words to change the situation. It's easy to talk about the problem and how it's not going to work out. "I just believe in telling it like it is. My back's been hurting for twelve years. I'll never get better. I've had this addiction since high school, and it's never going to change. The people I work with get on my nerves and always will." That's prophesying defeat. Do as this lady did and, in the midst of the difficulty, when you don't see any sign of it changing, dare to say, "All is well." You lost a loved one, and you should be depressed, but no, "All is well. God is still in control." You didn't get the promotion, and your friend says, "You deserved that promotion. That's not right." Don't join in and say, "You're so right. I can't stand my boss." No, "All is well. I know something better is coming." The medical report wasn't good. "Yes, but God is good, and all is well." You've been in a dry place, haven't seen any good breaks. "Yes, but I'm not worried. The abundance of rain is coming. All is well."

When the woman got to Elisha's house, she told him that her son had died. Elisha went with her and prayed for the boy, who came back to life. But I don't believe it would have happened if she would have sat around in self-pity and discouragement, thinking it was not fair. It happened because she dared to believe that "all is well" before she saw any sign of it. You may have a situation today that is not well. It may not be well in your finances, your health, or your relationships. In the natural, it's never going to change. You can choose to accept it, to get discouraged and complain about it, or you can choose to do as this woman did. In spite of what it looks like, in spite of what your mind tells you, and in spite of the negative reports, you can dare to say, "All is well."

Take Away the Enemy's Power

This is what the apostle Paul and Silas did in Acts 16. They hadn't done anything wrong, but they were put in prison and had just been beaten with rods. At midnight they were singing praises to God. They were saying, "All is well. We're not upset, we're not distraught, because we know God is still on the throne." Suddenly there was a great earthquake, the prison doors flew open, and their chains came loose. All was well.

Job went through a season of great trouble. He lost his health, his business, and his children. Everything went wrong, but he didn't get bitter. He said, "Though He slay me, yet will I trust Him." He was saying, "Whether it goes my way or doesn't go my way, all is well." If you're only going to be happy if everything happens your way,

> *If you're only going to be happy if everything happens your way, you're setting yourself up for disappointment.*

you're setting yourself up for disappointment. A mature attitude is, *All is well when my prayers get answered, and all is well when they don't. All is well when people are good to me, and all is well when they aren't. All is well when my dreams are coming to pass, and all is well when they're not.* You're not moved by your circumstances. That takes away the power from the enemy. If you don't have to have your way, he can't control you. You're saying, "God, my life is in Your hands. You know what's best for me."

Daniel was thrown into a den of hungry lions because he continued to pray to God rather than to the Persian king. His attitude was, *If I get eaten by lions, I'll go home to be with the Lord today. All is well. If not, I'm happy to stay here and finish my course. All is well.* The next morning the guards came in. I can imagine that Daniel was asleep over in the corner of the den. He was at rest. He wasn't worried. He knew that the enemy doesn't determine our destiny; God does. When you have an "all is well" attitude, you're not moved by the weeds. You're not upset over a disappointment. You don't lose your peace because somebody did you wrong. You don't live sour because a prayer didn't get answered your way. You know God is still on the throne, and He will get you to where you're supposed to be.

I read the story of a man by the name of Horatio Spafford. He was a wealthy businessman who lived in the 1800s. One night his wife and four daughters were on a ship crossing the Atlantic Ocean when their vessel collided with another ship, and all four of his daughters lost their lives. His wife sent him a telegram with the terrible news. A few weeks later, Spafford was traveling across the Atlantic to be reunited with his grieving wife. At one point the captain of the ship notified him that they were passing the exact location where his daughters lost their lives. That night he took out a pen and wrote these words: "When peace like a river attendeth my way, when sorrows like sea billows roll; whatever my lot, You have taught me to say, It is well, it is well with my soul." No matter what comes our way in life, we need to be able to say with him, "It is well with my soul. Life may have thrown me some curves, but it is well with my soul. All my dreams haven't come to pass yet, but it is well with my soul. I went through a divorce, but I'm not bitter, for it is well with my soul. I lost a loved one, and I may not understand it, but it is well with my soul."

Speak Faith to the What-Ifs

Over twenty years ago, my father went to be with the Lord. I received a call from my mother at 2:09 in the morning saying, "Joel, come over. Daddy's had a heart attack." He died the next day. It felt as though everything was out of control. I lost my best friend. We didn't know what was going to happen to the church. Would people keep coming? Who would be the pastor? There were all these variables. In the midst of that storm, with the winds blowing and the waves raging, our family could have worried and been depressed, but we had to do what I'm asking you to do. By faith we said, "All is well. God, You're still in control."

Sometimes you have to announce that "All is well," not just so you can hear it, not just so God can hear it, but so the enemy can hear it. He's expecting you to fall apart, get depressed, and give up on your dreams. But when you look that adversity in the eye and you're not moved by it, when you still have a smile on your face, when you still have a report of victory, when you're still being good to people, you give the enemy a nervous breakdown. He hit you with his best shot, but his best was not enough. He doesn't have the final say; God has the final say. He has not brought you this far to leave you. He's shown you His goodness, His favor, and His mercy in the past, and He'll do it again in the future.

> *Sometimes you have to announce that "All is well," not just so you can hear it, not just so God can hear it, but so the enemy can hear it.*

Now you have to do your part and speak faith into your destiny. If you don't talk positively to yourself, negative thoughts will try to talk you out of it. The what-ifs will bombard your mind. "What if it doesn't work out? What if the people don't come? What if your health doesn't improve? What if you never meet the right person? What if you don't have the finances? What if you don't make it?" No, declare by faith, "All is well. I may not see a way, but I know that God has a way. This may be a surprise to me, but it's not a surprise to God."

After my father died, I kept meditating on "all is well" for week after week, month after month. Today our family doesn't have to say it by faith alone. Today we can say that it is a fact.

Lakewood is strong. The future is bright. Our best days are still in front of us. All is well.

How you respond in the difficult times will determine whether or not you make it into the fullness of your destiny. If our family would have given in to self-pity, gotten discouraged, and said, "God, why didn't our prayers get answered?" we wouldn't be where we are today. There will be obstacles on the way to your Promised Land. We all have weeds in our

> *How you respond in the difficult times will determine whether or not you make it into the fullness of your destiny.*

field—things that don't make sense, things we don't like, losses, disappointments, unfair situations. Don't get sour, don't complain, and don't lose your passion. Do as Daniel did, do as the mother did with Elisha, do as the young couple did with the job and the house—have the attitude that all is well. That's showing God you trust Him. That's what allows Him to give you beauty for ashes and to take what was meant for harm and use it to your advantage.

The Promise Is Yours

You may be in a situation where you could easily be worried, upset, and give up on your dreams. You don't see how it can turn around. The prophet Isaiah says, "Say to the righteous that it shall be well with them." You are the righteous. God is saying this to you: "It shall be well with you." Not maybe, not I hope so, not if you get lucky—no, God promises it shall be well. Maybe you lost a loved one, and you don't think you can go on. It's not the end; it's a new beginning. It shall be well with you. If the job situation didn't work out, or you lost a client, let it go. God has something better. It shall be well with you. When you're struggling in your finances, and you don't see how you're going to make it, God has it all figured out. He is the Lord your provider. He clothes the lilies of the field. He feeds the birds of the air, and it shall be well with you. If the medical report wasn't good, God has another report. It says, "You will live and not die. The number of your days, He will fulfill. Nothing can snatch you out of His hands. It shall be well with you." Maybe you've been single for a long time, and you wonder if you'll ever meet the right person. Stay in faith. God has already lined it up, and it shall be well with you.

Now you have to do your part. Let this simple phrase play in your spirit all through the day: *All is well.* When you're tempted to worry, to get upset, to be discouraged, just smile and say, "No, thanks. I'm at peace. All is well." God has promised that all things—not some things, but all things—are going to work out for your good. That means even the weeds are going to work to your advantage. You may have some weeds in your life right now, situations you don't understand. Be encouraged. That's a sign you are close to your harvest. You're about to see a breakthrough, a healing, a restoration, a promotion. You may be saying it by faith today, but as the mother did with Elisha, one day you will say "All is well" as a fact. "All is well in my health, and I received a good medical report." "All is well in my career, and my dreams are coming to pass." "All is well in my marriage, and we're happy as can be." "All is well with my children, and they are fulfilling their destinies." You will see the faithfulness of God, dreams will come to pass, and His promises will be fulfilled.

CHAPTER TWO

Protect Your Peace

We should get up every morning believing for a good day, expecting favor, knowing that God is directing our steps. At the same time, we should realize that everything may not go perfectly today. Every person may not treat us right. Our plans may not stay on schedule. There may be some bumps in the road, things that we didn't see coming. If you're only going to enjoy the day if your plans work out, you're setting yourself up for disappointment.

In our cars, we carry a spare tire. When I drive somewhere, I'm not expecting to have a flat. I'm not expecting to hit a pothole that punctures the tire. I'm expecting to get to my destination as planned. But even though I'm expecting things to go my way, I've made provision in case they don't. I've taken steps ahead of time in case one of the tires goes flat. In the same way, even though you're expecting your plans to work out, even though you're expecting good breaks, you need to have your spare tire. You need to make provision in case things don't go your way.

How do you get your spare tire? At the start of the day you need to make a decision that no matter what comes against you, you're not going to get upset. No matter what someone says to you, you're not going to be offended. No matter what delays, disappointments, or bad breaks come your way, you're not going to be sour. You've already made up your mind to stay in peace. That's making sure you have your spare tire. If someone is rude to you, your attitude is, *No big deal. I'm not going to sit on the side of the road and sulk. I'm going to put my spare tire on and keep moving forward.* If you hit a pothole, if something unexpected happens—your loved one has an illness, your son forgot his homework, the loan doesn't go through—you could be upset or worried, but you have your spare tire. You decided ahead of time to stay in peace.

Always Carry Your Spare Tire

As good as the people in your life are, there are no perfect people. There is no perfect boss, no perfect friend, no perfect neighbor, and no perfect spouse. Victoria says that I am, but I know she's either lying or saying it by faith. Give people the room to be human. Quit expecting them to perform perfectly all the time. "Well, they hurt my feelings." If you have your spare tire, you forgive them and move on. Don't have unrealistic expectations for them. That person who loves you so much, no matter how good they are, at times will disappoint you. They're going to say things they shouldn't. Don't be easily offended. "Well, my husband didn't tell me he loves me today. This neighbor doesn't invite me over like she used to. My coworkers didn't congratulate me on my big presentation." You don't know what's going on in their lives. You don't know what they're dealing with. Don't take it personally.

Here's a key: Your happiness is not someone else's responsibility. You are responsible for your own happiness. Too often we're counting on other people to keep us cheered up, encouraged, and feeling good about ourselves. That's putting too much pressure on the people in your life. Let them off the hook. Nobody can keep you fixed except our heavenly Father. Don't go to other people for what only God can give.

> *Your happiness is not someone else's responsibility. You are responsible for your own happiness.*

Are you going through life without a spare tire, only happy if things go your way? The problem is, the roads are bumpy. There will be some potholes, some unexpected challenges. Without a spare, you'll get stuck on the side of the road—bitter over a breakup, upset because a coworker left you out, stressed over the traffic. Life is too short for you to live offended, upset, and discouraged. This day is a gift from God. We are not always going to be here. You have to put your foot down and say, "I am not going to let these same things keep upsetting me. I'm going to stay in peace. Even if the boss is unfair, even if my spouse is grumpy, even if my flight is delayed, even if the medical report isn't good, this is the day the Lord has made. I have made up my mind that I'm going to enjoy it."

When we go around offended, upset, and discouraged, it dishonors God. He has entrusted us with life. He could have chosen anyone to be here, but before time began, in His great mercy, He handpicked you. He not only chose you, but He created you in His own image. He's planned out your days, and He's crowned you with favor. Now He is directing your steps. The way to honor God is to get up every day with a passion to be your best and pursue what He put in your heart. Don't get stuck in the potholes of life. Shake off the offenses, shake off what somebody said, shake off the self-pity and bitterness. God saw everything that happened to you. He knows what was unfair. He knows how you were treated. Nothing is a surprise to Him. If you keep moving forward, He'll not only bring you out, but He'll bring you out better.

Tap into the Power to Remain at Peace

"Joel, I would stay in peace, but people at work don't treat me right. They're unfair, and they get on my nerves." You can't control what other people do, but you can control what you do. If you let them upset you, you are giving away your power and letting them control you. The Scripture says God has given us the power to remain calm in times of adversity. You don't have to let the same things keep upsetting you. Quit telling yourself, "I can't help it. They just know how to push my buttons." Try a new approach. Decide ahead of time that you're going to stay in peace, and you'll tap into that power to remain calm.

A man was walking down the street with his friend to buy a newspaper. They went into the corner store where the man bought the paper every

> *Quit telling yourself, "I can't help it. They just know how to push my buttons."*

day. The clerk behind the counter was as unfriendly as can be. He was cold, inconsiderate, and acted as though the man was bothering him. The man bought the paper, smiled, and said, "I hope you have a great day." The clerk didn't even look up to acknowledge what he said. His friend said, "Man, what was wrong with that clerk? Is he always that rude?" The man answered, "Every morning." The friend asked, "Are you always that nice?" He said, "Every morning." The friend looked puzzled and said, "Why?" The man replied, "I've made up my mind that I'm not going to let another person ruin my day." He was saying, "I have my spare tire. Yes, I hit this pothole every morning, but I'm not going to get stuck in an argument or be rude back to him and let him ruin my morning."

There may be people you see every day who have the gift of getting on your nerves. It feels as though their calling in life is to make you miserable. The good news is, you're in control. They can't make you unhappy unless you allow it. They can't make you be frustrated; it's your choice. Now, don't go the next thirty years letting the same things upset you, giving away your power. As this man did, make a decision that you are not going to let another person ruin your day—not the guy who cuts you off in traffic, not the clerk who's rude, not the family member who's disrespectful.

When someone is critical, condescending, and rude, they have unresolved personal issues that they're not dealing with. They've become poisoned, and now that poison naturally comes out. The key is to not let their poison get into you. Don't let their bad attitude sour your day. You overcome evil with good. You don't overcome evil with more evil. If you join in, and you're rude or you argue back, you've allowed their poison to contaminate you. But when you take the high road, when you rise above it and are kind to those who are unkind, when you're respectful when other people are disrespectful, then you're being an eagle. God will take you to heights that you've never imagined.

> *The key is to not let their poison get into you. Don't let their bad attitude sour your day.*

Don't Take the Bait

Years ago I promised a friend who works in a local news station that I would be on their program. I had to be at the station at 6:30 on a Monday morning. I woke up early that morning, and I was so tired. I didn't feel like going. It was cold and raining. But I had made the commitment, so I went. I was told to park inside the fence that was close to the station's main doors. It was still dark when I pulled into the lot, and there were no other cars there. I was about to park and get out, but a security guard came running over, waving both of her arms as though I had committed a major crime. She cried out, "What are you doing? You cannot park here. This is reserved for our special guests." I thought, *God, I'm going to need three spare tires for this lady. She's like a wrecking ball.* I said, "Ma'am, I'm on the program this morning. I was told to park here." She shot back, "Didn't you hear what I said? You cannot park here." I had to remind myself, *Joel, you're a pastor. Your church is right across the freeway.* I smiled and said, "That's fine." I drove out of the lot and parked on the street a few hundred yards away. It was still raining, so I had to run to the building. I did the program, and she must've seen it because afterward she came running up and said, "Oh, Pastor Osteen, if I had known that was you, I would've let you park there! Do you have time to pray for me?" I thought, *I would if I didn't have to walk so far.* I said, "Sure I will." I wanted to pray, "God, deliver her from that meanness."

What am I saying? Don't let another person ruin your day. Don't let a grouchy boss make you grouchy and then you take it home with you and are sour with your family. You can't keep it from happening, but you can keep it from getting inside. You have to guard your heart. Jesus says, "Offenses will come." He didn't say they might come. He didn't say that if you're a good person, if you're kind enough, and if you quote enough scriptures, then you won't have to

> *You can't keep it from happening, but you can keep it from getting inside. You have to guard your heart.*

deal with grouchy people, you won't hit any potholes. No, He says offenses will come. On a regular basis you will have opportunities to get upset, to live bitter and offended, to argue and try to pay people back.

The word *offenses* in the Scripture comes from a Greek word that means "bait." It's used in reference to how they would catch animals. It was actually the bait that lured the animal into the trap. When you're tempted to be offended, when somebody says something derogatory to you or they leave you out, recognize the enemy is offering you the bait. He's trying to deceive you into the trap. "Come on, get upset, be bitter, and argue back." Many people take the bait. They go around bitter, upset, and offended. The next time an offense happens to you, instead of letting those same things upset you, just say, "No, thanks. I'm not taking that bait. I'm not falling into that trap. I'm going to enjoy this day."

But it's easy to get baited into a conflict, to argue with people and try to prove our point. You have to be selective about which battles you fight. You're not supposed to engage in every conflict. If that battle is not between you and your God-given destiny, you should ignore it. Most of the things that come against us are simply distractions. Ask yourself, "If I win this battle, how will it benefit me? What will it accomplish? If I rush up to that car that cut me off in traffic and I cut them off, what will it gain me? I don't even know the driver. It's a distraction. If I'm rude back to the person who sold me the paper, yes, it makes the flesh feel good, but it doesn't put me further down the road. It's a distraction."

Only Fight the Battles That Matter

You need to choose your battles wisely. If you make the mistake of engaging in every conflict, straightening out coworkers, proving to other people who you are, you won't have time to fight the battles that do matter.

In the Scriptures, when David was a teenager, he was out working in the shepherds' fields when his father asked him to take a supply of food to his brothers. They were in another city serving in the army. When David arrived, he saw Goliath taunting the Israelite army, making fun of them. He asked some of the men there, "What is the prize for the man who defeats this giant?" They said, "The reward is that person will receive great riches, one of the king's daughters in marriage, plus they won't have to pay taxes." That got David's attention. He realized that was a battle worth fighting. There were big benefits. But when David's oldest brother, Eliab, heard him inquiring about fighting Goliath, he tried to embarrass David. In front of the other men, Eliab said, "David, what are you even doing here, and what have you done with those few sheep you're supposed to be taking care of?" He was trying to make David feel small, saying, "David, you are unimportant. You'll never do anything great." Now David had killed a lion and a bear with his bare hands. I have no doubt he could've taken care of Eliab. But the Scripture says David turned and walked away. One of the reasons that David did great things is he knew which battles to fight. He could've gotten into strife, arguing and trying to prove to Eliab that he was important. But if he had engaged in that conflict, if he had taken the bait, he would've gotten distracted, wasted time, and perhaps he would never have faced and defeated Goliath.

Are you fighting battles that don't matter that are also keeping you from battles that do matter? You have to learn to walk away from petty arguments. Walk away from disrespect. Walk away from jealous people. The writer of Proverbs says that avoiding a fight is a mark of honor—not winning a fight, but walking away from a fight. That's not being weak; that takes a strong person. That's a mark of honor.

> *The writer of Proverbs says that avoiding a fight is a mark of honor—not winning a fight, but walking away from a fight.*

In your marriage, you need to do all you can to stay in unity. It's easy to argue over every little thing, to live bitter and offended. The problem is, there will be some giants that you and your spouse have to face. On the way to your destiny, there will be Goliaths. That's how we go to new levels. But if you're distracted and arguing over little things, you won't be able to defeat those giants. You have to pass the test of biting your tongue, walking away when you feel like telling somebody off, overlooking an offense. The Scripture says one can chase a thousand, and two can put ten thousand to flight. When you're in agreement with your spouse, you are ten times more powerful.

When David was insulted by Eliab, he was able to bite his tongue and walk away. Do you know why? David prayed in

Psalm 141, "Lord, take control of what I say. Help me keep my lips sealed." He was saying, "God, help me to not say things I shouldn't. Help me walk away from rude people. Help me stay on the high road." Yes, it's good to pray for favor, to pray for wisdom, and to pray for protection, but I wonder how much further we would go if we would do as David did and start praying, "God, help me to shut my mouth." That's a powerful prayer. "God, help me to not say hurtful things. Help me to not be critical. Help me to not argue." When God can trust you to walk away from the Eliabs, from the people who are disrespectful, from the people who try to bait you into conflict, then He can trust you with the Goliaths. You will come into destiny moments when you will defeat giants that catapult you ahead.

Sit at the Table

As I've become more widely known, I've had more critics. Some of them were people who had large followings. When you hear negative things being said about you, especially things that are false or when your words are taken out of context, it's tempting to respond. But by the grace of God, I've always been good at letting these issues go. It's never bothered me in the least bit. I've learned that when I stay on the high road, when I don't try to prove to people who I am, when I don't live defensively, God will get me to where I'm supposed to be. It's been interesting that some of the people who were so against me don't have their platforms today. For some reason they have lost their following and influence. I'm not happy about that, but my point is that God

> *God will deal with the people who are trying to discredit you. It's not your job to straighten them out.*

will take care of the Eliabs. God will deal with the people who are trying to discredit you. It's not your job to straighten them out. Walk away from them and let God fight those battles.

David says, "God prepares a table for us in the presence of our enemies." When you have an enemy, that means God has a table for you. When someone's coming against you, when you have an Eliab at work who's trying to discredit you, recognize that there's a table there. You can go argue with them, you can be rude back to those who are rude to you, or you can sit at the table God prepared. When you sit, you're saying, "God, I'm trusting You to fight this battle. It's not between me and my destiny, so I'm not going to worry about the people at work who are trying to make me look bad. I'm going to keep honoring You, being my best. I know that while I'm seated at the table You prepared, while I'm in peace, You will take care of what's coming against me."

The apostle Paul did this. He had all kinds of opposition. Religious leaders didn't accept him, the government thought he had too much influence, and people lied about him. He was put in prison many times. He had plenty of opportunities to live bitter and offended. One place where we see his attitude is when he wrote to Timothy, "Alexander the coppersmith has done me great wrong, but God will repay him." He was saying, "That battle is not between me and my destiny. I'm not going to take the bait. I'm not going to get distracted. I'm going to sit at the table and let God fight my battles."

Are you fighting when you should be sitting? Are you trying to straighten somebody out and prove to them who you are? That's not your battle; that battle is the Lord's. You don't have to pay people back. You don't have to get even. God is your vindicator. He will make up for the wrongs that were done to you. If you stay in faith, stay in peace on that high road, God will vindicate you better than you can vindicate yourself.

Get Good at Ignoring

In 1 Samuel 10, the prophet Samuel chose Saul as the next king of Israel. Most of the people were happy and congratulated Saul, but when he returned to his hometown, some of the people who knew him the most weren't happy with Samuel's decision. They began to laugh and make fun of him. "Saul will never be our king. He doesn't have what it takes." The truth is, they were jealous of Saul. They were so insecure, so small-minded, that they thought they had to push Saul down so they wouldn't look bad.

Don't ever fight battles with small-minded people. Don't waste your time with people who are jealous, people

- *Don't ever fight battles with small-minded people.*

who don't value who you are, people who don't respect the anointing, the favor, and the talent in your life. Don't let them steal your peace. They are not between you and your destiny. If you engage in those conflicts, it will keep you from becoming who you were created to be. This is what it says Saul did:

"They despised Saul and refused to bring him gifts, but Saul ignored them."

If you're going to fulfill your purpose, you have to get good at ignoring things. Ignore negative comments, ignore disrespect, and ignore the naysayers—they don't control your destiny. They are distractions to try to keep you from God's best. Instead of being upset over who's not for you, frustrated over who's trying to make you look bad, do as Saul did and ignore it. Jealous people can't keep you from your destiny. Small-minded people cannot stop your purpose.

When Nehemiah was rebuilding the broken-down walls around Jerusalem, there were two leading men in that region, Sanballat and Tobiah, who didn't like him and opposed the work. They were constantly criticizing him, spreading rumors, at times shouting insults and making fun of him, trying to ruin his reputation. They were trying to bait Nehemiah into a fight and trying to dishearten the workers. But Nehemiah knew that they were not between him and his destiny. He didn't get upset or try to straighten them out; he simply ignored them. At one point they plotted to attack the city, but Nehemiah set up his defenses and refused to stop making progress on the wall. He went on to finish the wall in record time.

There will always be people who try to get you riled up. Don't take the bait.

When God puts a dream in your heart, there will always be Sanballats and Tobiahs who are critical, jealous, and disrespectful of you. There will always be people who try to get you riled up. Don't take the bait. That is not a battle you have to fight. They are distractions to try to get you off course, so you miss your purpose. Do as Nehemiah did and learn to ignore the Sanballats and Tobiahs. Your assignment is too important to be distracted by jealous, small-minded people.

Put On Your Shoes

In the Scripture, the apostle Paul tells us to put on the whole armor of God. One of the pieces of that armor is the shoes of peace. It's interesting that God chose our feet for peace. It implies that everywhere we go, we're going to have to choose to stay in peace. You can have on your helmet of salvation, your shield of faith, and your belt of truth, but if you don't put on your shoes of peace, if you don't make the decision that you're not going to get upset, you're not going to live offended, you're not going to get baited into conflict, then even though you have on all the other pieces of the armor, it's not effective without peace. Every morning you need to make sure you put on your shoes of peace. Too many people go through the day barefooted—offended, discouraged, and upset. But when you make the decision at the start of the day that nothing is going to upset you, you're putting on your shoes of peace. You're saying, "God, I trust You. I know You're directing my steps. Even if things don't go perfectly today, I believe all things are going to work out for my good."

When you're in peace, you're in a position of power. When you're upset, discouraged, and offended, it's just the opposite—you won't have the strength you need. The next time you're tempted to be offended, recognize what's happening and don't take that bait. When someone says something derogatory, instead of trying to pay them back, ignore them. Take a seat at the table God prepared. When you walk away from the Eliabs—the battles that don't matter—you will come into your Goliaths—opportunities that will thrust you ahead. I'm asking you to protect your peace. If you do this, I believe and declare you are not only going to enjoy your life more, but God is going to take care of what's coming against you. He's going to vindicate you, promote you, and take you to new levels of your destiny.

CHAPTER THREE

The Guardian of Your Soul

When we look at all that's going on in the world, it's easy to live worried and afraid. We watch the news and see natural disasters, sicknesses, accidents, and conflicts between nations. If that's not enough, now we're dealing with fears about pandemics. We think, *What if I get sick? What if my business doesn't make it? What if my child has an accident?* All these concerns are valid. If you were on your own, you would have a reason to live worried. But the Scripture says, "You have turned to your Shepherd, the Guardian of your soul." You are not in this by yourself. You have a protector, a defender, a deliverer. The Most High God is the Guardian of your soul.

When God breathed life into you, He didn't just put you on the earth and say, "Good luck. You're on your own." He said, "I'm going to guard you. I'm going to push back forces of darkness. I'm going to hide you from your enemies. I'm going to shield you from trouble." Psalm 91 says, "God rescues you from every trap and protects you from the fatal plague." You don't have to be afraid of a pandemic. God has a shield around you. He knows how to keep harm away. And if it does come, He knows how to heal you. He knows how to restore what was taken. He will rescue you from every trap. The enemy doesn't have the final say. Nothing can snatch you out of God's hand.

Because you turned to your Shepherd, He's protected you from things you know nothing about. He kept that car from hitting you. He pushed back sicknesses. He thwarted plans of the enemy and moved people out of the way who would have been a bad influence. He's been guarding your soul since you were born. If you knew all the things He's already kept you from, you wouldn't worry about what you're facing now. You would stay in peace, knowing that God has you covered. You're in the palms of His hands. You're not at the mercy of fate, bad luck, or a dreaded disease. You have a guardian, a protector, a God who promised He will rescue you from every trap.

When my father was a toddler, barely able to walk, his family lived on a farm. One night he wandered away from everyone and fell into a fire. He could have been killed easily, but it so happened that someone came walking by and pulled him out. Another fifteen seconds and he would have lost his life. That should have stopped his destiny, but there is a Guardian of your soul. There is a God watching over you who will rescue you from trouble. He will stop the plan of the enemy.

Psalm 121 says that your Guardian God is right by your side to protect you. He guards you when you go out, and He guards you when you return. He guards you now, and He will guard you always. You can't go anywhere without your Guardian God. That's why you can live from a place of peace, a place of faith, even though there's turmoil all around you. When other people are worried and panicked, stay in peace. It's not a surprise to God. He didn't say you wouldn't have trouble and have to face these things. But He did promise that He will rescue you from the trouble. He will keep the fatal plague from

> *You can't go anywhere without your Guardian God.*

taking you out. You don't have to worry about your future or be afraid of what could happen. God has a hedge of protection around you, a bloodline the enemy cannot cross.

The Distinction Put on You

After the Israelites had been in slavery in Egypt for hundreds of years, God told Moses that He was going to bring them out and lead them into the Promised Land. The way God did it was to send plagues on Pharaoh and his people who were oppressing them. What's interesting is that the Israelites lived next door, but none of the plagues affected them. God sent swarms of locusts that ate up all the Egyptian crops and destroyed their food supply, but right next door the Israelite crops were fine. I can imagine some of the locusts started to fly toward the Israelites' land, but when they got close it was as though they saw an electric fence and suddenly turned around and left the Israelite crops alone. This happened with plague after plague. God said in the book of Exodus, "I will make a distinction between My people and Pharaoh's people." At one point, all of

Pharaoh's livestock—his cattle, horses, donkeys, camels, oxen, and sheep—suddenly died. But right next door, the Israelite livestock was perfectly fine because God put a shield around His people. Even though the plague was all around them, He kept it from harming them.

As with the Israelites, because you belong to God, because you honor Him, He's put a distinction on you. What will defeat others won't be able to defeat you. When businesses are going down, you're going to go up. When others are struggling, you're going to be soaring. That's why David says, "A thousand may fall at my side, ten thousand at my right hand, but it will not come near me." David understood this principle that what happened to others wasn't going to happen to him. God put a distinction on him.

I don't mean this arrogantly, as though we're glad somebody else has difficulty and not us. I'm talking about living from a place of faith, knowing you have an advantage. God has a shield around you. Psalm 91 says, "God shields you from deadly hazards. Even though others succumb all around you, you will stand untouched. You will watch it all from a distance. Because God is your refuge, evil can't get close to you, harm can't get through the door." You may have some things come to the door, but it's not going to get in. You're going to come out

> *You're going to come out untouched.*

untouched. You're going to watch it all from a distance.

Years ago, the rapper MC Hammer had a popular song titled, "U Can't Touch This." You need to see yourself that way. When sickness comes, instead of accepting it and thinking, *I knew this would happen*, you need to announce to the enemy, "You can't touch this. I am God's property. My body is a temple of the Most High. I will live and not die." When lack and struggle come saying, "You'll never get ahead," just announce, "You can't touch this. The favor of God is on my life. I will prosper even in a desert." When your children aren't making good decisions and are getting off course, instead of being depressed and thinking, *What did I do wrong?* you need to remind the enemy, "You can't touch this. As for me and my house, we will serve the Lord. My children will be mighty in the land." You need to see yourself as untouchable to the enemy.

What Are You Saying?

We all have difficulties. I'm not saying that you won't have to face sickness, opposition, and betrayals. They may come, but they don't have to stay. You don't have to answer the door. Don't open it up and say, "I knew you'd show up. Come on in. Let me get you a cup of coffee." No, when they knock, say, "No, thanks. You're not welcome here." Don't accept it. Don't learn to live with it. Quit calling it *my* sickness, *my* anxiety, *my* dysfunction, *my* addiction. It's not yours. None of it belongs to you. It's on foreign territory. Your body is a temple of the Most High God. Sickness doesn't belong in your temple. Depression doesn't belong in your temple. Fear, addiction, and lack don't belong there. Stand firm and keep that door closed. Yes, things may come. I'm not telling you to deny the facts and to act as though you don't have a sickness. But you don't have to accept it in your mind. Don't let it become permanent, thinking it's always going to be that way. See it as temporary. This too shall pass.

I have several friends who contracted the coronavirus. They fought the good fight of faith and came through it. When you face a sickness, a bad break, or a loss, that doesn't mean you don't have this distinction on you or that you must not have enough faith. Not at all. The Scripture says, "Rain falls on the just and the unjust." There are times when difficulties come. We're praying and believing, but it didn't work out our way. When it rains, don't get discouraged. Don't give up on your dreams. God knows what He's doing. If you keep the right attitude, the rain is not going to hinder you; it's going to cause you to blossom. The enemy may have meant it for your harm, but the reason God allowed it is so He can bring you out better than you were before.

Psalm 91 opens by saying, "If you dwell in the secret place of the Most High, you will abide under the shadow of the Almighty." The next verse says, "I will say of the Lord, 'He is my refuge and my fortress; my God, in Him will I trust.'" It's significant that the psalmist didn't just say, "I'm going to stay in the secret place and that will keep me protected." He says, "I will say of the Lord." What you're saying is going to make a difference whether you see God's protection and favor in the way you should. "Joel, I'll

> *What you're saying is going to make a difference whether you see God's protection and favor in the way you should.*

probably get the flu or the new virus. I always have bad breaks. I don't think my business is going to make it. My children are never going to do what's right." You need to zip that up. You are opening the door to difficulties. If you're going to activate this protection, you can't go around talking defeat. You have to do as the psalmist did and start saying of the Lord, "Thank You that You are my Protector. Thank You that You are shielding me from every plague, rescuing me from every trap. Thank You that I'm going to come out of this untouched." The way you're going to see the distinction is by declaring you're protected and thanking God that there's a hedge around you.

David had all kinds of opposition. He had people trying to kill him. Armies came against him. His own son tried to dethrone him. He could have been afraid and complained, "God, You anointed me. Why am I having all these difficulties?" No, he kept coming back to a place of peace. Listen to how David talked in Psalm 27: "The Lord is my light and my salvation. Whom shall I fear? The Lord protects me from danger. Why should I be afraid? When enemies come against me, they will stumble and fall. Though an army surrounds me, I will remain confident. For in the time of trouble, God will hide me. He will place me out of reach, high on a rock." David knew how to activate this shield. You have to thank God for it. You can't go around worried and panicked and expect to see this hedge of protection.

Hidden from the Enemy

In 1 Samuel 23, David was on the run from King Saul. He had been good to Saul. He had been Saul's armor-bearer and served him faithfully. But Saul was jealous of David. He could see the favor on David's life. Saul couldn't handle the thought of someone getting more attention than him. So even though David had done nothing wrong, Saul was trying to kill him. He was so obsessed with it that he chased David again and again through the desert. Saul had the most skilled warriors. He had people who were specialists in tracking people. David, on the other hand, was a shepherd who didn't have any special training like Saul's men. Surely they could find David. Surely they could capture him. The Scripture says that Saul "hunted David day after day, but God did not let him be found." God knows how to hide you from the enemy. He knows how to hide you from trouble. He can hide you from a widespread virus. He will place you out of reach from the opposition.

> *He will place you out of reach from the opposition.*

Saul was so frustrated that he finally went back home. Later, some of the local men where David was hiding betrayed him. They contacted Saul's people and gave them David's location and all the details of where he was hiding. Saul was thrilled. He said, "Finally, someone has had mercy on me and will help me get rid of this man who's trying to take my throne." David wasn't trying to take Saul's place. Rather, Saul had disobeyed and not done what God told him to do, and now he was trying to take it out on David.

When you're doing the right thing and people are coming against you, trying to push you out, don't worry. That's not your battle. There is a Guardian of your soul. You have a protector, a defender. You don't have to fight. Stay on the high road, and God will keep you out of reach. He will hide you when you need to be hidden. He's not going to let that adversity stop your purpose. Don't live upset or afraid, trying to pay people back. Let God be your defender. He knows how to take care of the opposition.

Saul told the men who betrayed David to go back and spy on David—to study his movements and who he was with. Saul was so determined to catch David that he had them go overboard and do extensive surveillance. David didn't know that local men had betrayed him. He thought he was in a great hiding place. But at the last moment, David heard that Saul was quickly closing in. This time he was caught. There was no way he could escape. Saul was right on the other side of the mountain with all his army. It was just a matter of hours before David would be captured.

I can imagine David saying, "God, I didn't see this coming. I never dreamed those men would turn on me. But I believe that You will rescue me from every trap. I know that even though trouble surrounds me, You will bring me safely through." When he could have been panicked and given up, he kept thanking God for His protection. He kept thanking God that He would make a way where he didn't see a way. Right when Saul was about to give the command to make the final push, a man came riding on a horse as fast as he could. He had an urgent message for King Saul that said, "Hurry home. The Philistines are attacking our city." Saul called off the chase and told his men to turn around and go full speed to fight the Philistines.

God has ways to protect you that you've never thought of. He knows how to distract your enemies. He controls the universe. You don't have to figure out how it's going to happen. All you have to do is believe. "Lord, thank You that You are my protector. Thank You that You are my defender. Thank You that You are my way maker." When you realize the Most High God is guarding you, you can say with David, "I will fear no evil. I'm not going to fear a pandemic. I'm not going to fear this opposition. I'm not going to fear my future." You can stay in peace, knowing that the God who created the universe is the Guardian of your soul.

Your Power Position

Jesus says that in the last days there will be terrible epidemics, earthquakes, and famines. But don't panic or give in to your fears. An epidemic is a worldwide outbreak of disease like what we experienced with the coronavirus. That didn't surprise God. When you face difficulties such as that, He never leaves you. Choose to live from a place of faith, not a place of fear. When you're in peace, that's a position of power. When you know God is in control, you're going to be strong. You're

going to feel a force sustaining
you. But when you're upset and
afraid, that's going to drain
your energy, drain your moti-

> *When you're in peace,*
> *that's a position of power.*

vation, and your immune system is not going to be as effective
as it should be.

There is always a lot of negativity in the world. Many people are worried, afraid, and panicked. We all face threats to
our health and other challenges that are real, but don't let that
get in you. A ship doesn't sink because of the water around it.
It can be in a huge ocean, surrounded by hundreds of miles
of water on every side. The water around it is not a problem.
But when that ship lets what's on the outside get inside, it's a
problem. That means you can't watch the news all day and stay
afloat, so to speak. If you constantly take in negative news,
you're going to sink. I like to watch the news. It's important to
stay informed. But after fifteen minutes, I know what I need. If
you leave that television on all day, it's going to take six weeks
for you to get out of that pit. Tune that out, and tune in to what
God says about you. Don't let what's on the outside get inside.

The Scripture says, "Think on things that are pure, things
that are wholesome, things that are of a good report." Find
something to watch that's uplifting, something inspiring.
Think on things that build your faith. Don't call family members and friends and talk about the doom and gloom and how
bad it is. That's poisoning your spirit. You're feeding your inner
person by what you're taking in. If you're only feeding it the
negative, it's going to pull you down. One of the best things
you can feed yourself is what God says about you. "Lord, thank

You that my latter days will be better than my former days. Thank You that what You started in my life You will finish. Thank You that You are the Guardian of my soul."

Stay in the Secret Place

When I first started ministering in 1999, it was all very new to me. I had been behind the scenes doing the production for seventeen years. I was suddenly thrust in front of thousands of people. I never dreamed the ministry would grow and people all over the world would begin to watch. Then with the growth and notoriety came opposition from people who weren't for us. On top of that, I had the pressure of trying to learn how to minister. I wasn't sure if I was good at it. At one point, it felt overwhelming. It seemed as though there was opposition from every side. I wasn't sure how things were going to work out.

Then, in the midst of all that pressure, I had a dream one night. It was so vivid that I can remember it like it was yesterday. I was running through a field as fast as I could. There were planes flying very low overhead, dropping bombs all around me. It was as though it was right out of a war movie. I could see the bombs falling so close, and when they exploded, I would brace and wait for the shrapnel to hit me. One bomb hit fifteen feet away, and the explosion was deafening. When it hit, I knew it was the end. I was waiting to die. But every time a bomb exploded, somehow the shrapnel missed me. It happened four or five times in this dream. I was amazed I was still alive.

In my dream, after the bombs, I ended up running to a

little house. I was so afraid and hid in one of the rooms. I could hear soldiers running past, and I was hoping they wouldn't check the house. I was praying that they would keep going, but then my worst nightmare came true. They burst into the house, searching for me. Their guns were drawn, and I was standing right in front of them. I thought, *This is it. They found me. It's the end.* The soldiers looked right at me, then they turned around and walked out. It was as though I was invisible. When I woke up, I heard God saying in my spirit, "Joel, things may be exploding all around you, but I have you in the palms of My hands. Trust in Me, and no weapon formed against you will ever prosper."

Now when things come against me, and I start to be worried or afraid, I just remind myself that God is the Guardian of my soul. He has a hedge of protection around you. It is a bloodline that the enemy cannot cross. You may feel as though bombs are exploding around you—things that should stop your business, or damage your family, or harm

> *What you can't see is the Guardian of your soul is shielding you.*

your health. Don't worry. It's not going to be what it looks like. Those bombs are not going to take you out. It may be loud. It may seem as though you're done. What you can't see is the Guardian of your soul is shielding you. He's going to rescue you from every trap. God knows how to make you invisible to the enemy. The same God who made blind eyes see can make seeing eyes blind. He has all kinds of ways to protect you.

That's what happened to the prophet Elijah in 2 Kings 6.

The Syrian army had surrounded Elijah's house. The Syrian king was upset because God kept telling Elijah what the Syrians were going to do. What they discussed in secret, God revealed to Elijah. That way the Israelites always stayed one step ahead of them. When the Syrian king found out that Elijah was the informant, he was furious. He sent a huge army to capture him. When Elijah saw them coming, he said, "Lord, please make them blind," and He did. Elijah went out to meet them and said, "I heard you're looking for Elijah. You're in the wrong city. Follow me, and I'll take you to him." They didn't know it was Elijah. He led the Syrian army right into the middle of the Israelite camp. Then he prayed, "Lord, open their eyes and let them see." When they realized where they were and how they had been captured, they nearly passed out.

God has ways to protect you that you've never thought of. He can make you invisible to a virus, invisible to a person who's trying to stop you, invisible to the opposition. You don't have to figure it out. All you have to do is stay in the secret place. Stay close to God. Keep thanking Him that He's protecting you, that He's defending you, that He's the Guardian of your soul.

Be Untouchable

I read about a small fish called the Moses sole, a little flounder that swims in the same waters of the Red Sea as large sharks. The sharks typically like to eat these kinds of fish. In the early 1970s, a group of researchers noticed something fascinating about this little fish. All the other fish that were about the same size and weight were being eaten by the sharks, but not the Moses sole. It's because it has a very unique defense system. When it's in any kind of danger, its glands naturally secrete poisonous toxins. These toxins literally cause the shark's jaws to halt just as it is about to close its mouth over the sole. They showed a picture of this little fish swimming right in the middle of a shark's mouth. The shark had obviously come in for the kill. All it had to do was bite down, and there was dinner. But the shark couldn't do it. God put something in this little fish to protect it. As long as the shark was close, its jaws were frozen.

As with this small fish, God has put something on you that will keep the enemy from defeating you. What you're up against may seem bigger, stronger, and more powerful. Don't worry. It can't touch you. God has a hedge of protection around you. The way you release the toxins that cause the shark's jaws to freeze, so to speak, is by thanking God. Every time you say, "Lord, thank You that You are my shield. Thank You that You are my defender. Thank You that You are the Guardian of my soul," toxins are released that paralyze the enemy.

Now don't go around verbalizing your fears. "Joel, I'm worried about a virus. I'm afraid my child's going to get off course. My business is going to go downhill." Negative talk is like bait. It attracts the enemy. It will make things worse. The way you activate God's protection is with faith-filled words.

> *Negative talk is like bait.*
> *It attracts the enemy.*

Think about when that little fish is in the shark's mouth. Its blood pressure doesn't go up. It doesn't call 911. It doesn't get depressed and think this is the end. It just goes about its business. It knows there's something special about it—that God ordained from the foundation of the world that it would be protected from those enemies. So it just rests in the God who made it that way.

Get this down in your spirit: The Most High God is the Guardian of your soul. He put something on you that makes you untouchable to the enemy. You don't have to go through life worrying, afraid, wondering how it's going to work out. Live from a place of peace, a place of faith, knowing that your Guardian God is watching over you. If you do this, God has promised He will rescue you from every trap, protect you from every plague, and make you invisible to the enemy. Because God is your refuge, evil can't get close to you, and harm can't get through the door. You are untouchable.

CHAPTER FOUR

Peace with Yourself

We all make mistakes and do things we know we shouldn't. It's easy to go around with a heaviness, feeling badly about ourselves. But living with guilt doesn't do anything productive. It doesn't help you to do better; it causes you to struggle more. Guilt drains you emotionally. Physically, it will wear you out. When we're guilty, we don't pursue dreams. We don't believe we can overcome challenges. We get stuck.

This is why the enemy works overtime in this area. He knows that guilt will keep you from your destiny. There's nothing he would love more than for you to go through life being against yourself, focused on your failures, feeling unworthy. He's called "the accuser of the brethren." He'll remind you of everything you've done wrong for the last thirty years. Before you even get out of bed in the morning, your thoughts will replay mistakes that you've made—how you weren't there for your children, how you lost your temper, how you gave in to a temptation. Here's the key: The moment you asked God to

forgive you, He not only forgave you, but He doesn't remember
your sins anymore. That means if a voice is bringing up negative things from your past, that's not God. That's the accuser
trying to deceive you into carrying the heavy load of guilt. Do
yourself a favor and say, "No, thanks. I'm not perfect, but I am
forgiven." You can't drag yesterday's failures into today and live
in victory. Let it go. God's mercies are fresh every morning.
Don't spend another minute being down on yourself, living in
regrets. God has forgiven you.

> *You can't drag yesterday's failures into today and live in victory. Let it go.*

Why don't you forgive yourself?
God is not pushing you down.
Why don't you quit pushing
yourself down?

Be Bold as a Lion

The Scripture speaks of how God has made you righteous.
Righteous means "to be holy, blameless, honorable." It doesn't
say you're going to be righteous one day when you perform better or when you get your temper under control. You are righteous right now—not because of what you've done, but because
of what Christ has done. You can't do anything to make you
more righteous. In fact, the Scripture says all our righteousness
is as filthy rags, meaning that we can never measure up on our
own. No matter how hard we try to do what we know is right
or how disciplined we are, there will be times when we fail.

The apostle Paul says in the book of Romans, "The gift of
righteousness is for all who will receive it." If you see yourself

as unworthy, as undeserving, as not measuring up, the problem is that you're not receiving the gift. The accuser will tell you that you've made too many mistakes, you've failed too many times, and you'll never get it right. God says, "You are My holy, righteous, blameless, honorable, anointed, amazing child." Who are you going to believe? Are you going to let the accuser deceive you into carrying the guilt and going around being against yourself? Start receiving the gift.

Who are you going to believe?

When those voices remind you of everything you're not, of how many times you've failed, one of the best things you can say is, "I am righteous. I am holy. I am blameless. I am honorable." Everything in your mind will say, *No, you're not. You have an addiction. You keep giving in to the temptation. You made those mistakes.* But when you declare, "I am righteous," you are announcing to every force that's trying to stop you, you're announcing to the accuser, to the guilt, and to the heaviness, "You don't control my life. You don't determine my destiny. You can't stop my purpose. The Creator of the universe made me righteous. He made me holy and blameless." What are you doing? You're receiving the gift of righteousness.

Proverbs 28:1 says, "The righteous are as bold as a lion." When it comes to righteousness, you have to be bold. Your own thoughts will tell you, *You're not blameless. God is not pleased with you. How could He be? Look at what you've done. Look at your mistakes.* Guilt and condemnation will come knocking at the door. If you're unsure and doubtful, intimidation and guilt will take over. This is where you have to be bold. "I may not feel worthy, but I know that God has made me worthy. I don't feel righteous, but, Father, by faith I receive Your gift. I thank You that I am righteous."

"Well, Joel," you say, "I'm just an old sinner saved by grace." No, you used to be an old sinner, but when you gave your life to Christ, you became a new creation. Now you're not an old sinner—you're a son, you're a daughter, of the Most High God. You are a holy person, a righteous person, a blameless person, an honorable person. You may be carrying around a load of guilt with you now, but you might as well leave it right where you are. You might be weighed down with heaviness, with regrets, with a sense of unworthiness, but you can unload all that right now. You can make an exchange. If you give up your guilt, your regrets, and your unworthiness, God will give you His righteousness.

Lay Aside the Weights

Sometimes it's as though we're carrying all these heavy bags around. Everywhere we go, they weigh us down. Before we leave the house, we pick up a bag of guilt. Then we load up another bag with all the mistakes we've made, everything we did wrong, but there are so many that they won't fit in one bag, so we start to fill another bag. That bag still has some room, so we add in a long list of regrets. "I should have raised my children better. I should have finished school. I yelled at my coworker yesterday. Let me fit that regret in there. I lost my temper in traffic last week. I need a whole new bag for how

I've treated my spouse." We go through life carrying around all these bags, and we wonder why we walk with a limp. We wonder why life is a struggle, why we're tired, why we can't accomplish a dream. It's because we're carrying things we were never designed to carry. You weren't created to live with guilt, to have that nagging voice always telling you, "There's something wrong with you. You don't deserve to be happy." Those are weights the accuser uses to try to keep you from your destiny. If he can't get you off course, he'll at least try to weigh you down so you don't go as far as you should.

> *We go through life carrying around all these bags, and we wonder why we walk with a limp.*

The Scripture tells us to "lay aside the weights that can easily entangle us." It's easy to carry weights. Are you carrying weights of guilt? Weights of shame? Weights of regret? It's time to lay aside those weights. It's time to get rid of that baggage. Most airlines allow two bags per customer, but we need to have a very strict rule about guilt: no bags per customer. This is a new day. God wants you to go out lighter after you read this. The accuser has held you back long enough. Nothing you've done in the past is too much for the mercy of God. I believe chains are being broken and strongholds are coming down. You are redeemed. You are restored. You are holy. You are blameless. Shake off the guilt. Shake off the accusing voices and receive the gift of righteousness.

When our children were young, I took them to the toy store a lot. It didn't have to be a special occasion. I just liked to buy them things. I'd say, "Come on, Jonathan. Come on,

Alexandra. Let's go to the toy store!" Jonathan never once said, "No, Dad. I don't deserve to go. I didn't clean my room yesterday. I threw food at my baby sister." None of that came to mind. He simply said, "Yes, Dad. I'm ready. Let's go!" Children know how to receive a gift. They don't start debating whether or not they deserve it. Have they earned it? Have they been good enough? No, they just receive it as a gift. Like a child, you have to receive the gift of righteousness. Don't start thinking about all you did or didn't do, trying to figure out if you really deserve it, if you're good enough. You can't earn it. You'll never be good enough. It's a gift. Just receive it.

> *Children know how to receive a gift. They don't start debating whether or not they deserve it.*

The Price Has Already Been Paid

Sometimes we think we have to pay God back for our mistakes, and we try to do it by staying down and discouraged to show Him that we're sorry, that we're remorseful. Granted, there should be conviction and genuine remorse when we do something wrong. I'm not saying to just do whatever you want and never feel bad about it. My point is that once you ask for forgiveness, you don't have to pay God back. The price has already been paid. But when you live feeling guilty, you're saying, in effect, the sacrifice Christ made wasn't enough. You're saying, "Let me add something to it. Let me do my part by paying some kind of penalty for the wrongs that I've done." Living under guilt and condemnation doesn't bring any honor to God. After all Christ did to pay the price, if you want to honor God, get rid of the guilt. Quit listening to the accusing voices and move forward with your life.

The prophet Isaiah says, "God remembers our sins no more." God is all-knowing. He knows everything that's happened in the past, that's happening in the present, and that's going to happen in the future. But when we ask God to forgive us, this all-powerful, all-knowing God in a sense steps out of character and says, "I'm going to delete that event. I'm not going to keep any record of it." He chooses not to remember. If God forgets it, why don't you forget it? If God lets it go, why don't you let it go? I know people who ask God to forgive them for the same thing year after year, for something they did twenty years ago. They don't realize that the first time they asked God for forgiveness, not only did He forgive them but He doesn't remember it anymore. When you bring it up, it's as though God is saying, "What are you talking about? I don't remember that mistake. I don't remember the failure. I don't remember the time you gave in to temptation."

Quit remembering what God has forgotten. Quit telling Him how bad you are and how you messed up. He forgave you for losing your temper way back when you asked the first time. To keep bringing it up is only making you feel guilty, condemned, and badly about yourself. Instead of asking for forgiveness for the same thing, start receiving God's mercy. Mercy covers our mistakes. Mercy gives you what you don't deserve. You were guilty. It was your fault. You deserve judgment. But

> *Mercy covers our mistakes. Mercy gives you what you don't deserve.*

mercy says you're forgiven, you're redeemed, you're restored. When you're tempted to ask for forgiveness for the same thing, just turn it around and say, "Father, thank You for Your mercy in my life."

Get Back in the Game

This is what Jonah had to do. He had just made one of the biggest mistakes of his life. God told him to go to the city of Nineveh and tell the people to repent, but Jonah went in the other direction and almost lost his life. He spent three days in the belly of a great fish. When that fish finally spat him out on dry ground, you would think God would say, "Jonah, you need to sit on the sidelines and think about your mistake. You need to pay a penalty for that wrong. Maybe one day I'll use you again. Maybe one day I'll give you another chance to be a prophet." But as soon as Jonah was on dry ground, as soon as he was safe, the Scripture says, "The word of the Lord came to Jonah a second time, saying, 'Go to Nineveh, and tell them to repent.'" God was saying, in effect, "Jonah, you made a mistake. You got off course, but you repented. You asked for forgiveness, now get back in the game. You don't have to sit around defeated for a week, a month, or a year. I've forgiven you. Now go and do what I've told you to do."

A lot of times we categorize our mistakes by degrees. If it's a mistake we consider to be small, we think we have to pay God back by staying down and discouraged for a day or two. If it ranks as a mediocre mistake, we up the remorseful period to a week or two. But if it's something really big like Jonah did, where we really messed up and brought the trouble on ourselves, we think we have to give up our joy, our peace, and our dreams for at least a year or two. After all, it was our fault. But as it was with Jonah, God doesn't say to us, "Go sit on the sidelines and take a good long look at what you did. You blew it. You caused Me a lot of trouble. I'm not going to have anything to do with you for years." That's not the way God is.

Now the accuser will work overtime telling you, "God's not going to bless you. You can't expect His favor. You can't expect to accomplish any dreams. You owe God a whole lot for that mistake." No, the price has been paid by Christ. Don't believe those lies. I'm sure Jonah thought, *God, did I hear You right? You mean You still want me to go to Nineveh and tell them to repent? I just repented myself. I just got out of the fish that You sent to save me. Shouldn't I sit on the sidelines for a month and show You how sorry I am? Shouldn't I sit out at least a year and prove to You that I'll do what's right?* God said, "No, Jonah. I have something for you to do right now. I have an assignment for you. But as long as you are weighed down with guilt and condemnation, I can't use you to speak for Me. Shake off the guilt and go to Nineveh."

In the same way, God can't use you in the way He wants when you live feeling guilty, condemned, and down on yourself. We're not a good witness. We don't pursue dreams. We don't take steps of faith. God needs you to be confident, secure, and feeling good about yourself. He has an assignment for you.

Can you imagine what it was like when Jonah walked the streets of the great city of Nineveh and told them to repent? Every voice whispered in his ear, "Jonah, you're a hypocrite. You just repented days ago. You're no better than these people. You have no right to say a single word to anyone." Jonah had to do what we all must do. He had to ignore the accusing voices. He shook off the guilt and received the gift of righteousness. God was going to destroy the city of Nineveh, but because Jonah told them to repent, because he didn't sit on the sidelines trying to pay God back for his mistake, the whole city repented. Then God in His mercy changed His mind and spared over a hundred thousand lives.

> *Jonah had to do what we all must do. He had to ignore the accusing voices.*

Are you letting a mistake you made or a personal failure to convince you that God won't have anything to do with you right now? Are you thinking that maybe one day He'll use you, maybe one day He'll help you accomplish a dream? God is saying to you what He said to Jonah, "Get back in the game. Get your peace back. I have something for you to do right now. That mistake didn't stop your destiny. You don't have to sit on the sidelines of life. Start moving forward."

Sometimes when little children are misbehaving, their parents will give them a time-out. The child has to sit alone for a few minutes, during which there is no playing, no having any fun. We think that when we make mistakes, surely God must give us a time-out. Depending on how bad our mistake was, that's how long we think we have to sit out. We think God would have said, "Jonah, that was a big mistake. You caused

Me a lot of trouble. That's a five-year time-out. I'll see you way down the road." When you lose your temper, that's not to the level of what Jonah did, but you think you deserve at least a three-week time-out to feel guilty and condemned. When you give in to the same temptation for the fourth time in one month, that's a one-year time-out. But as it was with Jonah, God doesn't have any time-outs. He corrects us as His children, then He gets us on the right course and says, "Move forward." Now here's where you have to be bold, because thoughts will tell you, "You knew the right thing but you did the wrong thing. God's not going to bless you." Just say, "No, thanks. I've asked for forgiveness. I've received God's mercy. I'm not going to live condemned and be down on myself. I'm going to keep moving forward. I know I have a destiny to fulfill."

One More Time

In the Scripture, the birth of Samson was predicted by the Angel of the Lord, who told his mother that she would have a son, that he would be a deliverer and do great things. Samson started off well. He was given supernatural strength and couldn't be defeated by his enemies. But he let his guard down and started compromising. One thing led to another, and he made a lot of mistakes. This once powerful, influential man ended up losing his strength and being captured by his enemies. They gouged out his eyes, put him in prison, and he spent his days grinding at the mill. I'm sure the accuser said to him, "Samson, you blew it big-time. Even the angels said you would do something great, but look at you now. You're lower than a slave. You're in chains, working like oxen at the mill. You should feel guilty." You would think that because of all his poor choices that God would be done with him. After all, Samson knew better. It was his fault. But God never gives up on us. All those mistakes don't have to cancel your destiny. Don't believe those lies that you've gone too far off course, that you've made too many mistakes.

One day Samson's captors were holding a big reception in their temple. Several thousand people were there, and they brought Samson out to make fun of him. As he was standing there being mocked and ridiculed, he asked a young boy to place his hands on the two big columns that held up the temple. The Scripture says that Samson prayed, "O Lord God, strengthen me just this one more time." God gave Samson his strength back, and he was able to push over the columns, and the whole building collapsed on all the people who were in it. Samson defeated more enemies in his death than he had during his lifetime.

You may have made mistakes. The accuser is telling you that you're all washed-up. But as it was with Samson, God has a "one more time" for you. You have not seen your greatest victories. You have not sung your best song. You have not written your best book. You have not played your best play. You wouldn't be alive unless God had something amazing in front of you. Now the question is, will you get back in the game? Will you get your fire back, your passion back, your dreams back? Life is too short for you to go through it being down on yourself. You may have made mistakes. We all have. God is saying, "You're forgiven." Since He forgives you, why don't you forgive yourself? As long as you're beating yourself up, reliving failures, and dwelling on disappointments, that's going to keep you from your "one more time."

Shake that off. This is a new day. It's time to say good-bye to guilt, good-bye to condemnation, good-bye to heaviness.

Romans 8 says, "There is no condemnation to those who are in Christ Jesus," and here's the key: "who walk not after the flesh but after the Spirit."

> *As long as you're beating yourself up, reliving failures, and dwelling on disappointments, that's going to keep you from your "one more time."*

When you make a mistake, if you're in the flesh, you will beat yourself up and feel unworthy. You'll try to pay God back by staying down and discouraged. When you do that, you'll feel guilty, you'll feel condemned. But when you walk in the Spirit, you say, "Yes, I made a mistake. It was my fault. But I asked God for forgiveness, and I know that He not only forgave me, but He doesn't remember it. So I'm not going to sit around beating myself up. I'm saying good-bye to guilt. I'm saying adios to condemnation. I'm dismissing the accusing voices, and I'm getting ready for my one more time." That's when there's no condemnation, that's when you don't wallow around in defeat, that's when you don't believe the accuser's lies. You may have made mistakes. As with Samson, you got off course, but that is not how your story ends. If you shake off the guilt, God has a "one more time" coming your way. He has something bigger, more rewarding than you've ever imagined.

Wear a "Guilt-Free" Sticker

I've learned that just because you feel guilty doesn't mean you are guilty. You can't go by your feelings. Feelings don't always tell us the truth. I might not feel forgiven, but I know I am forgiven. I might not feel holy, and I know that I don't perform perfectly all the time, but I also know that I am holy, I am righteous, I am blameless, and I am honorable. You may ask, "Well, Joel, how can I say that?" You can say it because you have received the gift of righteousness.

The Scripture tells us to resist the enemy. To *resist* means to not agree with what he's telling you. When you hear him whisper, "You're all washed-up. You've failed too many times. You've made too many mistakes," the way you resist is to answer, "No, thanks. I know my best days are still in front of me. I know God's mercy is bigger than any mistake." Don't assist the enemy; resist him. He'll tell you, "You don't deserve to be blessed. Look what you've done." Instead of assisting him by saying, "Yes, you're right. What was I thinking?" resist him by declaring, "I am the righteousness of God. I am forgiven. I am redeemed." When the enemy says to you about your past, "Well, you failed, you blew it. You knew better and should have done better," talk to him about your future: "God's plans for me are for good. The path of the righteous, my path, keeps getting brighter and brighter. I know one more time is coming my way. Until then, I'm living in peace. I'm going to live guilt-free."

On the bag of my favorite chips is a sticker that says

"gluten-free." It means they don't have any gluten. You need to have an imaginary sticker on you that says "guilt-free," "condemnation-free," or "heaviness-free." When the accuser tries to dump that load of guilt on you, just show him your sticker. "Sorry, I'm guilt-free. Con-demnation is not acceptable here." When you picked up this book, you might not have real-ized it, but you entered a guilt-free zone. You're in a righteous

> *When the accuser tries to dump that load of guilt on you, just show him your sticker.*

place, a holy place, an honorable place, a hope-filled place, a one-more-time place.

Are you carrying some guilt that's weighing you down today? Are you assisting the accuser by believing his lies? It's time to start resisting him, to start believing what God says about you. We've all made mistakes, but remember that you don't have to pay God back. The price has already been paid. I'm asking you to receive His forgiveness, receive His mercy. You have enough coming against you in life as it is, so don't be against yourself. If you do this, I believe and declare the weights and condemnation are lifting off you right now. You're going to live guilt-free, confidently, securely, holy, blamelessly, righteously, and honorably in Jesus' name.

CHAPTER FIVE

God's Got This

We all have things that come against us. It's easy to live uptight, wondering how it's going to work out. What if the medical report isn't good? What if my finances don't get better? What if my child doesn't get accepted into that school? We've tried to figure it out, we've done our best, but we don't see anything changing. If we're not careful, we'll live worried and discouraged, not expecting it to get better.

But there's a simple phrase you have to keep down in your spirit: *God's got this.* He's on the throne. He sees what's happening. He already has the solution. You don't have to figure it out. There may not be a logical answer. In the natural, you don't see a way. That's okay, because we serve a supernatural God. He has ways to do it that we've never thought of. Instead of trying to force it to happen and living uptight, you have to let go and let God. When you turn it over to Him and say, "God, I know You've got this. I know You're in control," not only will you feel the heaviness, the weight, lift off you, but

God will make things happen that you couldn't make happen. Some of the things that are frustrating you now, causing you to lose sleep, will all change if you have this new perspective that God's got this.

Sometimes we're trying to play God. We're trying to make our boss promote us, or make ourselves get well, or make the contract go through. But as long as we're trying to force it, living frustrated and worried, God steps back. You need to take your hands off it and say,

> *Sometimes we're trying to play God.*

"God, I know You've got this. I'm not going to worry about my finances. I'm not going to live uptight because of the medical report. I'm not going to be frustrated because I haven't met the right person. God, I trust Your timing, and I trust Your ways. My life is in Your hands."

God never promised that we wouldn't have difficulties, but He did promise He will give us strength for every battle. He says He will take what was meant for our harm and use it to our advantage. You may have a good reason to worry about something, whether it's your health, your finances, or a dream. You've done everything you can. It doesn't look as though it's going to work out. Stay in faith. God is saying, "I've got this. I'm working behind the scenes. I'm in the process of turning it around. It's just a matter of time before you see things change in your favor." Now live out of a place of peace, a place of trust. It may not happen the way you thought, but God's ways are better than our ways. God knows what's best for you. He's got this.

Stay in Faith

In the Scripture, a wise older man named Daniel worked for King Darius. The Persian king loved Daniel, who was one of the three governors over the entire kingdom. Daniel was so good at what he did that the king was going to put Daniel in charge of his whole empire. But when the other leaders heard this, they were jealous and came up with a plan to get rid of Daniel. When you excel, when your gifts come out in great ways, don't be surprised if people get jealous. Everyone is not going to celebrate you. Some people will try to find fault and hold you back. The good news is, people don't determine your destiny; God does. Keep being your best, and let God fight your battles. Don't get distracted trying to prove to them who you are. God will be your vindicator. God will take care of your enemies.

> *When you excel, when your gifts come out in great ways, don't be surprised if people get jealous.*

The high officials who were against Daniel tried to manipulate the king. They said, "King Darius, you're so great! We've written a decree that no one can pray to anyone except you for the next thirty days. If they pray to any other god or man, they'll be thrown into the lions' den." They did this because they knew Daniel always prayed to Jehovah. They convinced the king to sign this decree, but that didn't change Daniel. Three times a day, just as he'd always done, he opened his windows, knelt down on his knees, and prayed to the God of Abraham, the God of Isaac, and the God of Jacob. When his enemies saw him praying, they ran back and told the king, "Daniel, who is one of the captives from Judah, is defying your order." The king was upset with himself. He realized they had manipulated him, but he couldn't go back on his legal decree, so he had Daniel sent to the lions' den.

What's interesting is that for a whole night the king fasted for Daniel and could not sleep. When you're in difficult situations, God has people praying for you that you don't know anything about. The king was supposed to be his enemy, but he was actually believing for Daniel's safety.

When they arrested Daniel and took him to the lions' den, he wasn't afraid, worried, or panicked. He understood this principle that God is in control. Many years earlier, Daniel had seen his Hebrew teenager friends, Shadrach, Meshach, and Abednego, get thrown into a fiery furnace and come out unharmed, without even the smell of smoke. Daniel's attitude was, *God's got this. I'm in the palms of His hands. Nothing can snatch me away. If it's not my time to go, I'm not going to go.* He stayed in peace. The apostle Paul says, "For me to live is Christ and to die is gain." He was saying, in effect, "If I live, I'm going to give God praise, and if I don't live, I'm going to give God praise. Either way, I'm going to stay in faith, knowing that God's got this." What you're facing may be bigger, stronger, and more powerful than you can handle. But when you refuse to worry, when you refuse to live stressed out and instead you stay in peace, thanking God that He's fighting your battles, knowing that He's in control, you are showing God by your actions that you're trusting Him.

The Mouths of Lions Close

On that evening when the authorities threw Daniel into the lions' den, they expected him to be eaten in a few minutes. These were hungry lions, and that's what always happened. But God supernaturally closed the mouths of the lions. For some reason they must have thought, *I'm not hungry tonight. I don't feel like eating.* One lion must have said, "Man, I'm full, too. I've got indigestion. I'm going to bed." God made Daniel unappetizing to those lions.

Have you ever sat down to eat, but when you looked at the food, you thought, *I'm not hungry for this*? I used to so love tuna sandwiches that I ate one every night. A few years after Victoria and I were married, I had a virus for a few days, and I was just getting over it when Victoria brought me a tuna sandwich. When I smelled that tuna, I almost threw up. I thought, *That is the worst smelling food in all the world*, even though I had been eating it every day.

I can imagine that when the lions looked at Daniel, they were confused and were thinking, *We should eat this man. We like a good steak dinner, but something is different tonight. We don't have our normal appetite.* God knows how to make you unappetizing to the enemy. What should normally take you out, what should normally defeat you—for some reason it can't harm you, it can't stop your business, it can't take your health. There is a bloodline that God has put around you and your family. God controls the universe. He controls the lions. He controls the enemies. You're not at the mercy of random events, or of people wanting to do you wrong, or of bad breaks.

> *You're not at the mercy of random events, or of people wanting to do you wrong, or of bad breaks.*

God has a hedge of protection around you. Nothing can happen without His permission. That's why we don't have to live worried or uptight. We're in a controlled environment.

When Daniel's friends, the Hebrew teenagers, were about to be thrown into the fiery furnace because they wouldn't bow down to King Nebuchadnezzar's golden idol, they said, "We know our God will deliver us, but even if He doesn't, we're still not going to bow down." They weren't panicked. They weren't upset or bitter. They knew they were in a controlled environment. They were saying what Paul said centuries later: "If we live, we're going to give God praise. If we don't live, we're going to go to Heaven and still give God praise." They stayed in faith, knowing that God has the final say. At some point we're all going to die, but I've made up my mind that I'm going to die in faith. I'm going to die believing, expecting, trusting, praising, smiling, and with a good attitude, knowing that God is in complete control. Nothing can snatch you out of His hands. The number of your days, He will fulfill. In life and in death, we have to know that God's got this.

Go Through It Without a Scratch

In the lions' den that night, Daniel wasn't uptight, sitting on edge and thinking, *I've made it this far, but any moment these lions could turn on me.* Animals can sense when you're afraid of them. But when you're calm, when you have your shoulders back and are confident, they know you're the authority. When we go hiking in the mountains, animal experts say, "If you see a bear, don't take off running. Don't panic. Don't lose your peace. Be still, be calm, and carry yourself with a quiet confidence." In the same way, when you face enemies in life— the enemy of sickness, the enemy of addiction, the enemy of debt—those enemies can sense when you're afraid of them. They'll take more ground. That's why the Scripture says, "Give no place to the enemy." But when they see you standing strong, thanking God when you could be complaining, being good to people when you could be bitter, at peace when you could be panicked, you are sending a message to those enemies that says loud and clear, "You have no power over me. You cannot stop me. My God is in control, and if He is for me, who dares to be against me?"

I can imagine that instead of worrying, Daniel found a nice soft patch of grass, lay down, and fell asleep. Early the next morning, the king came running to the lions' den to see what had happened. The Scripture says he called out in anguish, "Daniel, servant of the living God, has the God you constantly worship been able to save you?" Notice how he addressed Daniel, who was in the den because he was worshiping a different

God, yet the king called him, "Daniel, son of the living God." Even the king knew something was different about Daniel. When he saw Daniel come walking past the lions, unharmed, the king couldn't believe it. He was overjoyed. The Scripture says, "Not a scratch was found on Daniel because he trusted in his God." Amazing things happen when you stay in faith and trust God. He not only protected Daniel, but the king ordered the officials who'd conspired against Daniel to be arrested and thrown into the same lions' den. But they didn't have the same outcome. Before they hit the ground, the hungry lions

> *Amazing things happen when you stay in faith and trust God.*

tore them apart. The king issued a new decree that said, "From now on, everyone in my kingdom should worship the God of Daniel. He rescues His people. He's the living God."

Here's the key: God doesn't deliver us from every difficulty. Most of the time, He takes us through the difficulty. Daniel's faith didn't keep him out of the lions' den, but his faith did make him lion-proof. That's what brought him out of the lions' den. But if Daniel or if those Hebrew teenagers had been worried, panicked, and gotten negative, maybe there would've been a different outcome. Maybe we wouldn't be talking about them today. I'm asking you to quit worrying about what you're facing, quit losing sleep over that child who's not doing right, quit being upset because somebody did you wrong or your dream hasn't come to pass yet. Can I tell you that God's got this? As He did for Daniel, He's going to make a way where you don't see a way. As He did for the Hebrew teenagers, God's going to protect you, favor you, and get you to where you're supposed to be.

Live from a Place of Peace

David says, "Though I walk through the valley of the shadow of death, I will fear no evil." God is not just with you on the mountaintops. He's with you in the valleys when you're going through difficult things. He knows what you're up against. The Scripture says God is concerned about what concerns you. A sparrow doesn't fall to the ground without God knowing about it. How much more is God concerned about what's happening in your life? Trust Him. Live from a place of peace. This is a decision we have to make on a daily basis, because every day there's something to worry about. There's some reason to get upset. All through the day, keep this phrase close to your heart: *God's got this.* He's concerned about you. He's working in your life. He's bigger than your enemies. He's lining up the right people. He's arranging things in your favor. Your attitude of faith is what allows God to do amazing things.

When our son, Jonathan, was going off to college for his freshman year, as parents we were concerned about how it was all going to work out; would he meet the right people, would he get in the right classes? Because we travel a lot, our children were homeschooled, so he wasn't going to college with a bunch of friends, and he'd never been in a large classroom setting.

This particular college has 40,000 undergraduate students. It could have been overwhelming. Victoria really wanted him to meet somebody right at the start so he could have a friend or two. When she was at the parents' orientation on campus, she met a lady who said her son was in the Communications Department, as Jonathan was. She seemed like a nice lady, who had a great family. So Victoria texted Jonathan, who was in the students' orientation. She said, "Try to find a guy named Charlie. I just met his mother. I think you'll like him." Jonathan read the text and thought, *There are several thousand people in Communications, hundreds in this room alone. How can I ever find him?*

Going into a large room for his next session, Jonathan sat down on a random chair. The room was packed full of students. At one point the instructor told them to take a minute and meet somebody. Jonathan naturally turned to the guy sitting right next to him. Out of the corner of his eye, he could see a small name written at the bottom of this guy's notebook that said "Charlie." Jonathan looked at him and said, "I think my mother texted me about you. Are you Charlie?" This young man looked puzzled and said, "Yes, which means you must be Jonathan. My mother texted me about you." Out of the thousands of students, it just so happened they were sitting next to each other. You know what God was saying to us as parents? "I've got this. I'm in control. I'm going to watch over

> *Out of the thousands of students, it just so happened they were sitting next to each other.*

your children." Jonathan and Charlie became good friends, and eventually they sat next to each other at school for one last time as they graduated together. Charlie told Jonathan, "Let's finish as we started, side by side."

Are you worrying about your children, stressed out over your job, or discouraged because of a disappointment, thinking it's not going to work out? Come back to that place of peace. God's got this. He's directing your steps. He's bringing the right people across your path and your children's path. He has beauty for the ashes. Right now He's working behind the scenes in your life. Dare to trust Him. Dare to believe.

Victories Are Not Just for You

When we worry, we tie the hands of Almighty God. We all face situations that are bigger than us—a bad medical report, the loss of a major client, trouble in a relationship. It's easy to think of all the reasons why it's not going to work out. That's when you have to dig your heels in, switch over into faith, and say, "God, I know You've got this. Thank You for protecting my children. Thank You for fighting my battles. Thank You for healing my body." When you're tempted to worry, turn it around and thank God that He's working.

Daniel could have said, "God, I was doing the right thing. I was being my best. Why did this happen to me?" But sometimes God will allow difficult situations just to prove to you that He's God. He could have kept Daniel out of the lions' den.

He could have stopped the Hebrew teenagers from going into the fiery furnace. But God allows these things to not only show you, but to show others that He's God.

When David defeated Goliath, a giant twice his size, it wasn't just so David could be promoted; it was so David could be honored. That victory was a sign to the Philistines, a sign to all their enemies, and even a sign to the Israelites that God was in control and His hand of favor and blessing was on them. Some of the battles God allows in your life are not just about you. It's to make a statement to the people around you. Nothing speaks louder than when people see the favor on your life, when they see you overcoming obstacles that should have held you back, defeating giants that were bigger, accomplishing dreams when you didn't have the expertise. They will know you serve the true and the living God.

> *Nothing speaks louder than when people see the favor on your life, when they see you overcoming obstacles that should have held you back, defeating giants that were bigger, accomplishing dreams when you didn't have the expertise.*

Not only that, but when God brings us through the lions' dens and through the fiery furnaces, those victories are like fuel to feed your faith when you face other challenges. You'll know that if God did it for you back then, He'll do it for you again. Don't get discouraged when you face things you don't understand, obstacles that are bigger than you. That's simply an opportunity for God to show you who He is. It's one thing to believe that God has power, to believe that He can do the impossible. That's good, but God wants you to do more than just believe. He wants you to experience His power. He's going to show you His greatness, to show you His favor.

Surrounded by Favor

David had all kinds of things come against him—not just giants and armies, but his own family. He had plenty of reasons to live worried, afraid, and bitter. But he says in Psalm 27, "The Lord is my light and my salvation; whom shall I fear? The Lord protects me from danger; why should I be afraid? When people come against me, they will stumble and fall. Though a mighty army surrounds me, my heart will know no fear. Even if they attack, I will remain confident." David lived with this attitude: *God's got this. I'm not going to be worried. I'm not going to live upset. I know He's bigger than any obstacle I'm facing.*

A few verses later, David added, "When trouble comes, God will hide me. He will place me out of reach, high on a rock." You may have enemies coming against you, but you have an advantage. God has placed you out of reach. They can't defeat you, and they can't keep you from your destiny. Now do as David did and remain confident. Keep your peace. It may feel as though you're surrounded by an army. The truth is, you are surrounded by God's favor. The forces for you are greater than the forces against you. David says, "Even if they attack, I won't get upset." Sickness may have attacked you, addictions may have attacked, debt may have attacked. That's a test. Are you going to get worried and live in fear? Are you going to think, *What if it doesn't work out? Did you see the medical report? There are 40,000 students, so what if my child doesn't meet the right people?* Stay in peace. Remain confident. God has done it for you in the past, and He's going to do it for you again in the future. In a few verses, David says, "I am confident I will see the goodness of God." After all he'd been through, you would think he'd be negative and worried, saying, "God, where were You?" He was just the opposite. His attitude was, *I know I'll see God's goodness.* In other words, *I know God's got this.*

I talked to a lady recently who had been through a divorce and was carrying all the hurt and pain. She never dreamed her life would turn out as it had, and she was confused and discouraged, wondering why it happened. One day while driv-

> *Let go of the old.*

ing in her car, she felt God say to her, "I still have a good plan for your life. Let go of the old. I've got this." At that moment she made the decision to stop worrying, to stop being down on herself. She let it go. Suddenly, it was as though a heavy weight lifted off her. She got her joy and passion back. Now new doors are starting to open, new relationships, new opportunities. She's starting to see the beauty for ashes. It all happened when she changed her perspective.

Is something weighing you down today? Are you worried about a situation, frustrated by what didn't work out? Or maybe you're down on yourself because you're not where you thought you would be. God is saying to you what He said to her: "I've got this. It's not a surprise to Me. I have new beginnings. I have healing. I have breakthroughs. I'm asking you to change your perspective. Switch over into faith." That situation at work that you're worried about—God's got it. That medical report that's keeping you up at night—living stressed out by it is not making it any better. Be still and know that He is God. He has you in the palms of His hands. He's got this. You may have enemies coming against you, but God has placed you out of reach as He did David. He's made you lion-proof as He did Daniel. Now all through the day when you're tempted to worry, keep this phrase playing in your mind: *God's got this.* If you do this, you're going to see God's goodness in new ways. You're going to come out of the lions' den, rise higher, accomplish dreams, and become everything God created you to be.

CHAPTER SIX

It's Already Set Up

It's easy to go through life worried about how we're going to accomplish a dream, or how we're going to get out of a problem, or how we're going to meet the right person. We look at all the reasons why it's not going to work out, but when God laid out the plan for your life, He lined up everything you need to fulfill your destiny—every good break, every person, every solution. He's not trying to figure out how to do it. It's already set up. He's already set up the promotion. He's already set up the healing. That problem you don't think will turn around, He's already set up the answer. It's not a surprise to Him. He had the solution before you had the problem. There may be things that you're dreaming about, desires God put in your heart that seem so unlikely today. God wouldn't have given you the dream and not made a way to bring it to pass. It's already in your future waiting for you, and if you stay in faith and not let negative voices talk you out of it, you'll come into what God has already set up.

In Luke 22, the Passover was approaching, and Jesus was about to be crucified. He told Peter and John to go ahead of Him to Jerusalem and make arrangements for their Passover meal, which is now known as the Last Supper. They asked Him where they were to go. He told them that as soon as they entered the city, a man would meet them carrying a pitcher of water. He would lead them to a certain house, and they were to ask the owner where the guest room was, where He could have the Passover meal with His disciples. The Scripture says, "The owner will take you upstairs to a large room that is already set up." Jesus didn't say, "Go to the house and tell them that Jesus wants to have dinner. Quick, get it set up. Get the food. Get the table." He said, "It's already set up." What God has planned for you, He's not thinking about doing it. It's not that maybe one day it will happen, one day He'll bring it together. It's already in place. And the good news is, God knows how to get you there.

Notice how detailed Jesus was. He said, "As soon as you enter the city, you'll meet a man—not just any man, but a man carrying a pitcher of water. He will lead you to a house. Tell the owner what I need, and he'll take you upstairs." It was like a movie. All these details had to come together at exactly the right time. If the man in the city would have been late, the disciples would have missed him. If he hadn't been carrying a pitcher of water, they wouldn't have known who to follow. If he led them to the wrong house, nothing would have been prepared. It was the right person, the right house, and the right timing. Everything fell precisely into place.

What am I saying? God is not only strategically directing

your steps, He's orchestrating everything around you. He has the people you need who will be there not just to meet you, but they will lead you to your blessing, lead you to a promo-

> *It was the right person, the right house, and the right timing. Everything fell precisely into place.*

tion, lead you to the next level. Peter and John didn't have to convince the owner to be good to them. "Please do us a favor. Jesus really wants to have dinner here tonight." The owner was expecting them. He already knew they were coming. He had the table already set up. God has some of these already-set-up blessings waiting for you. He's already spoken to the right people to be good to you. He's lined up divine connections, people who will go out of their way to show you favor. You don't have to try to manipulate people and force a door to open. God has already prepared the hearts of the people He has ordained to help you. They'll have the table already set up.

It's Going to Come to You

I know a man who went to a government office to get some paperwork that would allow his business to grow. The clerk behind the counter was very unhelpful, very rude, seeming to be annoyed. He took the man's information, but he told him that they were so backed up that it could take five years for the paperwork to go through. The man was very disappointed; nevertheless he asked nicely, "Is there anything you can do to speed it up?" The clerk almost yelled at him, "Sir, I told you that we're backed up! It's going to take five years." The man left that office discouraged. Two weeks later, the clerk called and said his paperwork had gone through and was ready. The man was excited, went back to the office, saw the clerk, and thanked him. He said, "I thought you said it was going to take five years." The clerk said to him, "It should have, but ever since I met you, I can't get you off my mind. I wake up thinking about you, I eat dinner thinking about you, and I go to bed thinking about you. I'm sick of thinking about you. Take the paperwork and leave."

When God has ordained someone to help you, they don't have to like you. Quit being frustrated by who's not for you. If they're supposed to be for you, they'll be good to you even though they don't like you. They can't help it. God controls the universe. If He needs them to play a part in what He's already set up for you, they won't have a choice. The Scripture says, "God has purposed it. Who can annul it?" This is saying, "What God has already set up, who can stop it?" People can't stop it. Bad breaks can't stop it. Injustice can't stop it. It's already set up. You are right on schedule. You keep honoring God, and what He's already set up is going to find you. You're not going to have to go after it. It's going to come to you.

> *People can't stop it.*
> *Bad breaks can't stop it.*
> *Injustice can't stop it.*

When we needed land to build a new sanctuary, twice the properties that we really wanted were sold out from under us. I was disappointed. I thought, *God, where are You?* I didn't realize the Compaq Center was already set up. When it doesn't work out your way, it's because God has something better. Don't live frustrated. The doors are closed because God is doing us a favor. Six months later, a friend of mine called out of the blue and said, "Joel, let's go to lunch. I have an idea." He told me that the Rockets were moving out of the Compaq Center and how it would be a great home for Lakewood. In one sense, I didn't go after the Compaq Center. The Compaq Center came after me. God used my friend to lead me to what He already had prepared. He was a divine connection, part of the plan that God had already set up.

That's why you don't have to live worried. You don't have to wonder how you are going to accomplish the dream, how you're going to get the breaks you need. God has it all figured out. He's already lined up the right people to come across your path, and what God has in store is bigger than you can imagine. It's more rewarding and more fulfilling. Instead of going around discouraged because of what didn't work out, turn it around and say, "Father, thank You for the blessings You've already set up. Thank You for the good breaks, for the healing, the promotion, and the right people You've already ordained to come across my path." When you live in faith, expecting God's goodness, there will be moments of favor that you suddenly come into. You didn't see it coming. There was no sign of it, but suddenly the paperwork goes through. Suddenly the Compaq Center shows up. Suddenly you meet the right person. That was one of those blessings God had already set up.

Destiny Moments

In Mark 11, Jesus was on the Mount of Olives. He told two of His disciples to go into the nearby village, and they would find a young donkey tied up, which had never been ridden. Jesus said, "Untie it and bring it to Me. If anyone asks what you're doing, tell them the Lord needs it and will return it soon." They went into the village and found the colt just as He'd said. As they started to untie it, somebody stopped them and demanded, "What are you doing? That's not your animal." They said, "The Lord needs it," and they were given permission to take it. Jesus got on the colt and rode it into Jerusalem, and when people saw Him coming, they put palm branches down on the ground and laid out their coats. As He passed by, they shouted, "Hosanna! Blessed is He who comes in the name of the Lord!" This was all prophesied by the prophet Zechariah hundreds of years earlier, that Jerusalem would receive their king coming on a colt that had never been ridden.

But when the disciples went to get the colt that day, they didn't realize the significance of what they were doing. They thought they were just running an errand. Jesus needed a colt to ride, no big deal. They didn't know the colt they were untying was fulfilling biblical prophecy. It seemed routine to them, but there was nothing ordinary about that moment. They couldn't see it, but it was part of a plan that the Creator of the universe had already set up.

> *They didn't know the colt they were untying was fulfilling biblical prophecy.*

As with them, there are times we're going through the day, doing our normal routine, going to lunch with an old friend who called, no big deal. We can't see it, but those are destiny moments. God is orchestrating what He ordained for your life to come together. As Zechariah prophesied that Jesus would come riding on a colt, your life has been prophesied. God has written every day of your life in His book. You are not at the mercy of people, luck, or "I hope I get some breaks." Before you were formed in your mother's womb, God knew you and planned out all your days. He has these destiny moments where He'll make things happen that you can't make happen. He's already set up the colt. He's already set up the table. He's already set up the right people and the breaks you need. Not only are your steps being divinely orchestrated, but He's orchestrating the steps of people and circumstances around you. If He knew where that colt was, if that animal was put there by the Creator, how much more does God know where you are? How much more is He lining up what you need?

That colt had never been ridden. It had been kept to fulfill Zechariah's prophecy. I can imagine that when the owner had tried to ride it as he did his other animals, he got halfway on the colt and got bucked off. He thought, *I'll show you*, and he had four or five strong men hold the colt, but when he tried to get on, it was as if the colt had supernatural strength and bucked him off again. He finally thought, *I'm leaving that colt alone. Something's wrong with it.* But there wasn't anything wrong. That colt had been marked by destiny.

One thing this shows us is that what God has ordained for you will not go to anyone else. Don't worry about somebody getting your promotion, your contract, or your blessing. If it's yours, that colt will buck them off. What God has prophesied for your life cannot be taken by other people. Now quit being frustrated because somebody got what you wanted. If it was supposed to be yours, that wouldn't have happened. Be happy for them, knowing that God has something better for you. When we tried to buy that property for a new sanctuary, that colt bucked us off twice. Even though I did my best to make it happen, I couldn't override what God had ordained. Just as God opens doors that no person can shut, God closes doors that no person can open. Don't lose your peace because something bucked you off. Be wise enough to realize that God didn't want you to have it. If it's supposed to be yours, you can rest assured that nobody else will get it.

> *Just as God opens doors that no person can shut, God closes doors that no person can open.*

The Right People in the Right Positions

When the prophet Samuel went to Jesse's house to anoint one of his sons as the next king of Israel, seven of the sons were in the house. Jesse didn't bother to bring in his youngest son, David, who was still out in the shepherds' fields. He thought, *David's not king material. He's too young, too small, and doesn't have the talent or the experience.* People will judge you by the outside. They'll try to write you off, but they don't know what

God put in you. They can't see your seeds of greatness. They didn't prophesy your life. They didn't choose you before you were formed in your mother's womb. They don't know what God has already set up for you. God loves to take people others discount and discredit by saying, "It couldn't be them. They're not king material. They've made too many mistakes. They come from the wrong family." That's the kind of people God chooses to show out in their lives.

Samuel called each of the sons of Jesse to come forward one by one, and I can imagine him trying to pour the oil to anoint them, turning the bottle upside down, but the oil wouldn't come out. When Samuel came to the seventh son, I can see him hitting the bottom of the bottle, but the oil defying gravity because it was not ordained to go to any of those seven sons. The oil that belongs to you will not go to anyone else. Nobody got your promotion. Nobody got your contract, your girlfriend, or your house. The oil that belongs to you cannot go to other people. Jesse finally brought in David, the youngest son. Samuel went to anoint him, and the oil freely flowed. I can see his father standing there with his eyes and his mouth wide open, thinking, *David? I never dreamed it would be him.*

What God has already set up for you is going to cause people to stand there in total disbelief, as Jesse did. They never dreamed you could be that blessed, that successful, that healthy, or that free. They only saw you with all your limitations, what you couldn't do, what you didn't have. They didn't realize God had already set up blessings that would catapult you to the next level. The Scripture says, "No person has seen, heard, or imagined what God has prepared for those who love Him." God

> *God has some things prepared that are going to amaze you, promotion that you won't see coming, favor that you don't deserve, increase that takes your family to a new level.*

has some things prepared that are going to amaze you, promotion that you won't see coming, favor that you don't deserve, increase that takes your family to a new level. If you've seen it, heard it, or imagined it, that's not what this is talking about. What God has prepared, what He's already set up, is something you've never seen.

In 2007, we received a phone call from a young lady who worked for the New York Yankees. We'd never met her, but she liked our ministry. The Yankees were building a new baseball stadium. She wanted us to come and hold a Night of Hope for the first event in the new stadium. When the staff told me, I thought they were joking. "You mean that they want a minister from Texas to come?" They could have had a big rock-and-roll band or some other big production, but she wanted us. This young lady was in charge of special events. She could have liked us, but she could have been working in accounting or on the grounds crew. There's nothing wrong with that, but she wouldn't have had the authority to invite us. So in 2009, we went and held the first non-baseball event in the new Yankee Stadium.

What am I saying? God has the right people in the right positions for you. You don't have to have favor with everyone, just favor with the right one. A dozen people may not like you, but they can't stop you. God has already set up the right

people who will open doors to
promotion, to opportunity, to
favor. You're going to say as I
did, "Wow! I didn't see that
coming. I didn't have the con-

> *You don't have to have favor with everyone, just favor with the right one.*

nections, the talent, or the experience." That's one of those prepared blessings that you have not seen, heard, or imagined.

Don't Get Talked Out of It

Sometimes there's a blessing already set up, but people will try
to talk you out of it. People will tell you all the reasons why
it's not going to happen. The problem is, God didn't put the
dream in them; He put the dream in you. They can't see what
you see. They can't feel what you feel. They're looking at it in
the ordinary, the natural, but God puts things in your spirit
that are bigger than you can accomplish on your own. You may
not see how it can happen, but God wouldn't have given you
the dream, He wouldn't have put the promise in you, if He had
not already set up how to bring it to pass. He's a supernatural
God. He knows how to bring it all together. He has the colt set
up. He has the staff members who like you in the right position. He has the table already prepared.

When I was growing up, my mother always wanted a
swimming pool in our backyard. My father was very generous
with my mother. It seemed like he would give her anything,
except a swimming pool. He said, "Dodie, I don't want a pool.
It's too much money and too much maintenance. We already

have enough to take care of." He gave her all these good reasons, but my mother paid no attention to that. She let that go in one ear and out the other. Every day she went around saying, "I can't wait till we get our swimming pool." She got all five of us kids excited and saying, "We're getting a swimming pool!" We even went out and bought my brother, Paul, some floaties. My father said, "Dodie, you are wasting your time. I've already made up my mind. We are not getting a swimming pool."

One day my mom was in the backyard with a tape measure. My dad went out and asked, "Dodie, what are you doing?" She said, "I'm measuring where we're going to put our swimming pool." She tried to wear him down, but he wouldn't budge. About a year later, after a service during our Thanksgiving Conference at the church, a couple asked to see my parents. They introduced themselves, and the man said, "I build swimming pools for a living." My mother gave him a big hug and said, "I've been waiting for you." He went on to say, "I would like to build you a swimming pool." My father said, "That's so nice of you. You're very kind, but we really can't afford it right now." The man said, "What do you mean? I don't want you to pay. I want to do it for free. Won't you let me give you a swimming pool?" My mother gave my father a look that said, "If you say no, you're going to Heaven today." That man built us a beautiful swimming pool in our backyard.

That was one of those blessings God had already set up. My father couldn't see it, but God didn't put it in his heart. Don't let people talk you out of what God put in you. Just because they don't believe doesn't mean it's not going to happen. God has lined up the right people for you, and if you keep honoring Him and being your best, these blessings are going to find you. Don't seek the blessing; seek God. Keep Him first place, and the blessing will seek you. Jesus says, "Seek first the kingdom, and all these things will be added to you." These things are what God has already prepared. He wants to not only meet your needs, but He wants to give you the desires of your heart. He wants you to enjoy life and be able to bless your family and have fun together.

"Well, Joel, it's great your mom got her swimming pool, but I'm fighting cancer." "I'm struggling with an addiction." "I have a child who's off course." The same God who had a swimming pool already set up for my mother, the same God who had the Compaq Center already set up for us, and the same God who had a colt already set up to bring Jesus into Jerusalem has the healing already set up for you. He has the vindication, the freedom, the breakthrough. Keep your peace, and get ready. It's already in your future.

The Answer Is Already on the Way

In the Scripture, when Joseph's brothers were jealous of him, they threw him into a deep pit and were going to leave him there to die. But just then they saw a caravan of Ishmaelite merchants coming their way. They changed their minds and decided to sell Joseph as a slave to the traders. What's interesting is that this caravan had been traveling for months on the way to sell their goods in Egypt. Before Joseph was thrown into the pit, God had the answer already on the way. Before he had

> *"Before you call, I will answer you."*

the problem, the solution was already en route. God said in the book of Isaiah, "Before you call, I will answer you."

I saw a report on the news about a mother who was driving in the car with her two small children over a very high bridge. An eighteen-wheeler lost control of his truck and started a chain reaction, slamming into cars. This lady's car was not only crushed, it was pushed through the guardrail, halfway off the bridge. Now it was dangling on the edge, rocking back and forth. When the police arrived, the car was so mangled they didn't think anyone had survived. They radioed that they had fatalities, but then they heard something coming from inside the car, just a little noise. Somehow the people were still alive, but the car was so unstable. For about ten minutes they tried to cut through the metal to get them out, but they had to stop. It was too risky. Every time the wind blew, it looked as though the car was going to fall. The officers knew they didn't have long, but they didn't know what to do.

Just then a man in a Navy uniform came walking up. He said, "I'm the head of a Navy engineering team, and we have a one-of-a-kind forklift that can extend out, tilt, rotate in any direction, and lift eleven thousand pounds." The officer said, "How quickly can you get it here?" While they were talking, it pulled up. The forklift would be able to reach out, pick up the car, and save the three lives. After they rescued the people, the Navy engineer told the police officers that earlier that day they had been delayed for three hours. They should have already been to their destination, but something caused them to be late. It just so happened that they were coming by when all this was taking place. What are the chances of this one-of-a-kind piece of equipment being at that place at the right time? That wasn't a lucky break. It wasn't a coincidence. It was one of those blessings that God had already set up.

God knows what you need, when you need it, and how to get it to you. That problem you're concerned about, God has the answer already en route. Instead of worrying all through the day, you need to say, "Father, thank You that You've already set up the breakthrough, already set up the promotion." Everything you need to fulfill your destiny is already lined up. It may not have happened yet, but if you stay in faith, what God has ordained is on the way. You're about to come into some of these already-set-up blessings. You're not going to have to go after it. It's going to come after you.

> *God knows what you need, when you need it, and how to get it to you.*

QUESTIONS FOR GROUP DISCUSSION

Chapter One: All Is Well

1. What difference does having an "all is well" attitude make?

   _____

   _____

   _____

   _____

2. When you see a difficulty springing up, instead of losing your peace and falling apart with discouragement, what should you do?

   _____

   _____

   _____

   _____

3. How did Daniel represent the power of "all is well" when he faced the lion's den?

   _____

   _____

   _____

   _____

Chapter Two: Protect Your Peace

1. If you are going to stay in peace with imperfect people, what do you need to realize about them, and how do you need to be prepared to respond to them?

   _____

   _____

   _____

   _____

2. How does going around offended and upset dishonor God? What is the way to honor Him and move past what keeps you stuck?

   _____

   _____

   _____

   _____

3. What areas do you find yourself most vulnerable to being baited into conflict? What truths do you need to tell yourself to protect your peace?

   _____

   _____

   _____

   _____

Chapter Three: The Guardian of Your Soul

1. We all have difficulties. Sickness, opposition, and betrayals may come, but they don't have to stay. How is it possible to keep the door closed when they knock?

   _____

   _____

   _____

   _____

2. When you feel fear and panic, what can you remind yourself to keep anchored to peace?

   _____

   _____

   _____

   _____

3. Living in a world that's like an ocean of negativity around us, what steps can you take to keep the water from coming into your boat?

   _____

   _____

   _____

   _____

Chapter Four: Peace with Yourself

1. Reflect upon the heavy bags that you are conscious of carrying right now. What impact are they having on your daily life?

_____

_____

_____

_____

2. What is it like to receive the gift of righteousness as a child receives a gift?

_____

_____

_____

_____

3. After you have made mistakes and you feel washed-up, how do you get your passion back, your peace back? What truth will you tell yourself to get back in the game?

_____

_____

_____

_____

Chapter Five: God's Got This

1. "God's got this." When you face a difficult situation, is this truth about God firmly rooted in your heart? What change in your thinking will help you improve in this area and stay in peace?

_____

_____

_____

_____

2. What reason does the Scripture give to explain how it was possible for Daniel to leave the lions' den without a scratch? What encouragement does this give you about your faith?

_____

_____

_____

_____

3. When God brings you through difficulties, how does He use it to fuel your faith when you face other challenges?

_____

_____

_____

_____

Chapter Six: It's Already Set Up

1. We all face something that we can't see how it's ever going to work out, how we'll get the breaks we need. What is that thing in your life, and what truth about God will keep you from being frustrated?

   _____

   _____

   _____

   _____

2. The colt that Jesus rode had never been ridden before. It had been kept to fulfill Zechariah's prophecy. What does this show you about what God has ordained for your life?

   _____

   _____

   _____

   _____

3. Describe a time in your life when someone tried to talk you out of something that God put on your heart. Did you stay in faith and see it come to pass?

   _____

   _____

   _____

   _____

ACKNOWLEDGMENTS

In this book I offer many stories shared with me by friends, members of our congregation, and people I've met around the world. I appreciate and acknowledge their contributions and support. Some of those mentioned in the book are people I have not met personally, and in a few cases we've changed the names to protect the privacy of individuals. I give honor to all those to whom honor is due. As the son of a church leader and a pastor myself, I've listened to countless sermons and presentations, so in some cases I can't remember the exact source of a story.

I am indebted to the amazing staff of Lakewood Church, the wonderful members of Lakewood who share their stories with me, and those around the world who generously support our ministry and make it possible to bring hope to a world in need. I am grateful to all those who follow our services on television, the Internet, SiriusXM, and through the podcasts. You are all part of our Lakewood family.

I offer special thanks also to all the pastors across the country who are members of our Champions Network.

Once again, I am grateful for a wonderful team of professionals who helped me put this book together for you. Leading them is my FaithWords/Hachette publisher Daisy Hutton, along with team members Patsy Jones, Billy Clark, and Karin Mathis. I truly appreciate the editorial contributions of wordsmith Lance Wubbels.

I am grateful also to my literary agents Jan Miller Rich and Shannon Marven at Dupree Miller & Associates.

And last but not least, thanks to my wife, Victoria, and our children, Jonathan and Alexandra, who are my sources of daily inspiration, as well as our closest family members, who serve as day-to-day leaders of our ministry, including my mother, Dodie; my brother, Paul, and his wife, Jennifer; my sister Lisa and her husband, Kevin; and my brother-in-law Don and his wife, Jackelyn.

We Want to Hear from You!

Each week, I close our international television broadcast by giving the audience an opportunity to make Jesus the Lord of their lives. I'd like to extend that same opportunity to you. Are you at peace with God? A void exists in every person's heart that only God can fill. I'm not talking about joining a church or finding religion. I'm talking about finding life and peace and happiness. Would you pray with me today? Just say, "Lord Jesus, I repent of my sins. I ask You to come into my heart. I make You my Lord and Savior."

Friend, if you prayed that simple prayer, I believe you have been "born again." I encourage you to attend a good Bible-based church and keep God first place in your life. For free information on how you can grow stronger in your spiritual life, please feel free to contact us.

Victoria and I love you, and we'll be praying for you. We're believing for God's best for you, that you will see your dreams come to pass. We'd love to hear from you!

To contact us, write to:

Joel and Victoria Osteen
PO Box #4271
Houston, TX 77210

Or you can reach us online at www.joelosteen.com.

Stay connected, be blessed.

Get more from Joel & Victoria Osteen

It's time to step into the life of victory and favor that God has planned for you! Featuring new messages from Joel & Victoria Osteen, their free daily devotional and inspiring articles, hope is always at your fingertips with the free Joel Osteen app and online at JoelOsteen.com.

Get the app and visit us today at JoelOsteen.com.

 **JOEL OSTEEN** MINISTRIES

CONNECT WITH US

....
....
....
....
....
....
....
....
....
....
....
....
....
....
....
....
....
....
....
....
....
....
....
....
....

"Sometimes when you face challenges, it's not because
you're doing something wrong, but because you're
doing something right."

....
....
....
....
....
....
....
....
....
....
....
....
....
....
....
....
....
....
....
....
....
....
....
....
....

"Your happiness is not someone else's responsibility.
You are responsible for your own happiness."

....
....
....
....
....
....
....
....
....
....
....
....
....
....
....
....
....
....
....
....
....
....
....
....
....

"He will place you out of reach from the opposition."

....

....

....

....

....

....

....

....

....

....

....

....

....

....

....

....

....

....

....

....

....

....

....

"You can't drag yesterday's failures into today and live
in victory. Let it go."

....

....

....

....

....

....

....

....

....

....

....

....

....

....

....

....

....

....

....

....

....

....

....

....

....

"Amazing things happen when you stay in faith and
trust God."

....
....
....
....
....
....
....
....
....
....
....
....
....
....
....
....
....
....
....
....
....
....
....
....

"You don't have to have favor with everyone, just favor
with the right one."